Shame Regulation Therapy for Families

Uri Weinblatt

# Shame Regulation Therapy for Families

## A Systemic Mirroring Approach

Springer

Uri Weinblatt
Systemic Mirroring Family Therapy Institute
Modi'in, Israel

ISBN 978-3-030-08463-9 ISBN 978-3-319-77470-1 (eBook)
https://doi.org/10.1007/978-3-319-77470-1


Softcover re-print of the Hardcover 1st edition 2018


Printed on acid-free paper

This Springer imprint is published by the registered company Springer International Publishing AG part of Springer Nature.
The registered company address is: Gewerbestrasse 11, 6330 Cham, Switzerland

# Introduction

What is common to all of the following experiences?

- A child plays a game with a friend and loses. He explodes, aggressively throwing the game board to the ground.
- An adolescent girl wants to be friends with two other girls. When they reject her, she goes and cuts her arms.
- An adolescent boy who has been asked by his parents to stay home, rather than go out, curses at them and yells "I'll do what I want!"
- A mother requests that her son clean up his room. When she enters his room for the third time, she screams and yells and tells him that he is a terrible son.
- A father decides to stop talking to his daughter because she is disrespectful.
- A wife requests that her husband arrive home earlier. When he arrives late, she yells "you never cared for me! You only care about yourself!"
- A student is requested to make a presentation in class. On the day of the presentation, he stays at home.
- A teacher tells a student to open his book. He refuses and says, "Who are you to tell me what to do?" The teacher reacts by sending him out of the classroom.
- In a teacher–parent conference, the teacher tells the parents about their child's low grades. Soon both sides start blaming each other for the child's situation.

While we usually do not understand these diverse life events to be representing a common experience, they can all be viewed as expressions of shame. Indeed, the word shame does not capture the many human experiences that are fueled by the emotion of shame. Instead, we use other words (such as: aggression, hurt, pain, acting out, disrespect, humiliation, uncaring, shyness, power struggles, and low self-esteem) to describe them. Yet, all these words are either triggers for or behavioral consequences of the experience of shame. They are all connected with a disruption in the ability to collaborate, an experience of being exposed as inferior, not worthy or uncared for, and they all lead to predictable reactions – blaming the other, blaming ourselves, or withdrawing.

Shame, more than any other emotion gives us the answer to the following question:

> *"Am I important to you?"* (Do I have value? Do you care about me? Do you see me? Do you like what you see?)

When the answer is yes, we experience a range of feelings which contradict, prevent, and oppose shame – a sense of worth, a sense of being loved, a sense of pride, a sense of belonging, and a sense of closeness. When the answer is no, we experience shame – we feel unappreciated, worthless, insignificant, humiliated, and alone.

As adults, we are not supposed to be dependent on the evaluation of others. We are expected to be self-sufficient creatures that can provide for ourselves the approval, admiration, and respect we need. Admitting how important it is for us to be appreciated by others is shameful and often evaluated as childish and needy. Dependence has become a negative word, a pathology, something we fear. Yet, for shame to be regulated, we need others. Tragically, the more shame we have, the more we need others, but are less able to admit it.

Mark Twain has remarked that "In his heart no man respects himself."[1] Occasionally, we all experience shame which leads us to blame, criticize, and dislike ourselves. At such moments, we need others to free us from the shaming process in which we are both perpetrator and victim. We need others to remind us that we are not so awful or complete failures. We need others to reassure us that even if we made a mistake we are still decent human beings and that even if we are not perfect we are still loved.

## A Different Kind of Empathy

Carl Rogers was the first great therapist to tackle shame. Although he did not relate to shame directly, it is he, more than any therapist before him, who understood the significance of enabling clients to have a voice – that is, to be able to relate to their experience and to communicate it fully to another person, without being judged. Roger's focus on the self, and on its relationship to itself and others, has led him to develop a radical new model for the therapeutic relationship. In this encounter, the traditional shaming practices of psychoanalysis which were common at the time, namely, the structure of wise Doctor – ignorant patient, blaming patients for not agreeing with the doctor, and basing therapy on interpretations, were revised. Patients became clients, the therapeutic relationship became more equal, the therapist adopted a position of not knowing more than the client and instead of blaming (or interpreting) client's behaviors, clients received empathetic reflections. Since then, empathy became the great antidote for shame, and the empathic climate was shown to be the best environment for exposing the fragile self to the beneficial warmth of others.

---

[1] *Following the Equator*, Pudd'nhead Wilson's New Calendar.

Indeed, empathy is a powerful force in the amelioration of shame, and yet, it has limits. The leading two are:

- Empathy can increase shame.
- Empathy has little influence on people who are highly avoidant and uncooperative (as a result of too much shame).

Therapists of all orientations discover that approaching high shamed (shame prone) individuals, couples, families, and organizations with classical empathy as a primary tool can lead to failures which intensify the shame in the system. Ironically, empathy can make the shamed person feel worse about himself – his defensive reactions to others' positive and kind gestures only make him look (in his own eyes and in the eyes of others) bad, ungrateful, and mean. In addition, the empathetic attitude also demands exposing one's self, which can easily lead to an intense shame reaction.

Let's look, for example, at a short transcript taken from the first moments of the first session with Mia, an 18-year-old adolescent girl who was referred to our therapy center after two unsuccessful psychotherapies. This is a part of the conversation she had with one of our therapists who is known for her openness and warmth:

Therapist: (warmly, starting with small talk) "Did it take you a long time to get here today with all this rain?"
Mia: "Why do you want to know?"
Therapist: (still pleasantly) "I just hope it didn't take too long, anyway I am glad you are here."
Mia: (silent)
Therapist: (trying to connect) "I heard you have tried therapy twice. Was it hard to come in again?"
Mia: "No."
Therapist: (gives compliment) "I think that coming in again demands courage, I respect that."
Mia: (becoming withdrawn, looking away)
Therapist: (puzzled) "Did I say anything that upset you?"
Mia: (more withdrawn)
Therapist: "We don't need to talk about that."
(Uncomfortable silence)
Therapist: (trying again) "So tell me, how would you like therapy to look this time?"
Mia: (getting angry) "Like nothing."
Therapist: "Nothing?"
Mia: "Yes, is there a problem with that?"
Therapist: "I was just interested in understanding what your expectations…"
Mia: (interrupting) "I have no expectations!"
Therapist: (trying to show empathy) "O.k., that is fair. If I were you, I would probably have no expectations either."
Mia: "Stop thinking you know how I think!"
Therapist: "I am sorry if I offended you…"
Mia: "You didn't offend me. You see? You are doing it again; you think you know who I am!"

The simple empathy-joining strategies failed and the effort to connect with Mia led to more impasse. The same held true for the compliments that caused her to become withdrawn and disconnected. It seems like the process of trying to understand and show compassion toward Mia lead to distress and interruptions in the process of developing a relationship with her. This progression is typical for people referred to as "shame prone," meaning that they can easily experience shame in a very intense and painful way. With such individuals "trying to understand" can generate frustration for all people involved. This, however, does not mean that communication is impossible. Let's look at what happens in the conversation with Mia once the therapist does something else –

Therapist: "You are right, I can see that I was talking as if I know you."
Mia: "So why did you do that???"
Therapist: "I don't know, I guess that sometimes it's helpful."
Mia: "Well it's not helpful for me!"
Therapist: "I get it. Thanks for letting me know; I will try not to do it again."
Mia: "o.k."
Therapist: "o.k."
Mia: (looking for a moment at the therapist, cautiously smiling) "What else did you want us to talk about?"

While the shift the therapist made does not seem dramatic, it leads to a conversation which is of a different quality. What did the therapist change? She stopped interacting in ways which elicit shame and instead acted in ways which reduce shame, in this case admitting her mistakes, admitting her misunderstandings, and giving up the position of being above Mia. The therapist shifted her orientation from what I call a "low shame state" in which shame is regulated, to a "high shame state" in which shame is under regulated. How did she know she had entered into a high shame state? By observing Mia's reactions. In high shame states, questions, reflections, and expectations not only fail to develop a positive rapport (where they would have succeeded in low shame states) but actually promote and propagate an adversarial climate. Once the therapist identified that she had entered into a high shame state dynamic, she did something different. It is empathy, but of a different kind.

## The Power of the System

As the example shows, the limits of classical empathy interventions are evident with highly avoidant individuals. For example, children and adolescents who experience high levels of shame and exhibit a range of problems – aggressive behaviors, school refusal, academic failures, and various social problems – are notorious for not responding well to therapy. Actually, many of them will never step into a counseling room, and even when they do, the results are typically counterproductive. They will often be diagnosed as either depressed or as having different oppositional/behavioral problems. The main under-regulated emotion – shame – will not be addressed directly, and its impact on the child's life will remain misunderstood. With such kids, empathy alone will not help them to escape the shame-avoidance loop that they got caught in. What such kids need is a system to heal their pain. They need others to mirror their abilities, strengths, and hope, and they need the power of their social network (family, community) to shift them from their avoidant position.

Shame is the most public emotion. It is in the presence of other people (real or imagined) that we experience the most shame, and it is with the help of others that we can alleviate our shame. The most important of these others are our family members. Unfortunately, it is often in the family that we do the most shaming and are most often shamed.

In families and other systems (such as school), shame will frequently be addressed under the disguise of disrespect. The more disrespected we feel, the more shame we feel. Actually, many power struggles in families are hidden efforts to regulate shame:

Mother: "David, can you please clean your room."
David: (playing on the computer) "Just a second."
Mother: (5 minutes later, starting to feel disrespected) "I told you to clean your room three times. Can you just go and do it?!"
David: (feeling disrespected) "I told you I will do it. Why do you always have to interrupt me?!"
Mother: "Because you never do anything when you are asked to do it!"
David: "If I never do anything anyway, then I won't do it now either!"

The conversation can continue and escalate in different directions, leading to name calling, punishments, and alienation – actions which will only intensify shame in the system.

Similar dynamics often occur in schools. Teachers and students engage in various power struggles which are fueled by shame, but are viewed as conflicts stemming from disrespect:

Teacher: "Open your notebook please, and copy what I wrote on the blackboard."
Student: (ignores)
Teacher: "Can you please write like the rest of the class?"
Student: "No I can't."
Teacher: "Open your notebook, NOW!"
Student: "You open your notebook!" (Class laughs, teacher feels shame).

While the two examples can be viewed as displays of disrespectful behavior, they can also be seen as efforts to regulate shame. When children experience a demand or command, it immediately makes them feel inferior. Both are unaware of their shame, and do what most of us do when we are shamed – we make the other feel shame. However, in the second example, we see an additional shaming factor. The presence of other students in the class amplifies the shame of the teacher, and it is what makes the student's remark so devastating. The system has the power to reduce shame, and it can also become the leading agent in a shaming process.

## The Emotion of Intimacy

Just as shame is the most public emotion, it is also the most private and hidden emotion. When we feel shame, we wish to hide and not be seen. We wish to prevent anyone (including ourselves) from exposing that which is hidden. Yet, the more we try to maintain secrets from ourselves and others – the more we experience shame.

For shame to be regulated, it needs to be exposed. We cannot break out of our shame without allowing ourselves and others to see who we are.

Client: "I need to tell you something, but I also can't tell you."
Therapist: "What will happen if I find out?"

Such discussions are common with people who experience shame. The dilemma of exposing one's self is ever present and needs to be managed constantly.

For relationships to become close, people need to uncover their shame. Confiding feelings of inferiority, failure, unattractiveness, stupidity, or of being "bad" create potentials for successful shame management. When this potential is actualized we experience intimacy. When communicating shame is done in a nonconstructive way – we find ourselves in a fight.

## Mirroring All Realities

This book is intended for therapists, counselors, and educators who are involved in regulating the shame of children, parents, couples, and teachers. The importance for addressing shame rests on two basic assumptions: the first is that at the heart of many problems that brought the client/clients to therapy (child acting aggressively, heated escalations between couples, communication problems between parents and teens or between partners, school problems, etc.) lies unregulated shame which leads to intense suffering for the individual and his or her environment. The second assumption holds that most of the disruptions in the therapeutic relationship are shame related. Thus, just as shame plays a dominant role in regulating relationships in the client's life outside therapy it also regulates the quality of the therapeutic relationship. As a result, without the continual regulation of shame in the therapeutic encounter, the most sophisticated and good willed interventions offered to clients are at best used minimally and at worst intensify shame, thus leading to rejection of the interventions and to conflict and resistance in the therapeutic relationship. Interestingly, it is often after shame has been regulated that clients suddenly do not need specific interventions to solve their problems, and rather, without the paralyzing presence of shame, can use their own resources, knowledge, and abilities to find practical solutions to their problems.

In the book, I deal with relationships in different contexts: parents and children, teachers and students, therapists and children or adolescents, and others. Moreover, I often switch from talking about one type of relationship (for example, parent–child) to another (therapist–parents) – this, in order to emphasize the common processes that shame gives rise to in a variety of relationships. Some chapters, however, focus on the distinctive aspects of regulating shame in specific contexts.

The aim of the approach presented in this book is to provide a therapeutic framework that deals with the two major challenges of shame regulation:

- The challenge of addressing both the individual and relational aspects of shame: while shame is commonly perceived as an extremely private emotion, it is in fact also very public, in that it strongly influences, and is influenced by, the reactions of others. Thus, an effective therapeutic approach needs to combine individual and systemic/relational interventions in a way that both makes sense and feels safe to the client.
- The challenge of adjusting to states of shamelessness and shamefulness: different levels of shame call for different relational strategies. An effective shame-regulation approach needs to respond flexibly to the varying intensities of shame, while maintaining therapeutic integrity and cohesion. This means that, in some cases, the therapist's goal is to reduce shame while in others to increase it.

To meet these challenges, I have integrated and further expanded two highly effective therapeutic models: a parent training model and a couple therapy model – namely, Nonviolent Resistance (NVR) and Collaborative Couple Therapy (CCT), respectively. These I tailored to working with children and adolescents. While neither approach puts shame at the center of attention, both contain powerful interventions for the regulation of this emotion.

NVR (Omer 2004) is a parent-training approach originally developed by Haim Omer for empowering parents and reducing acting-out behaviors in children. One of Omer's great achievements was constructing a powerful therapeutic model that is not dependent on the child's collaboration for success and which leads ultimately to much more cooperative and respectful family dynamics. I have been implementing this model in therapy from its inception and found that its various interventions are effective in regulating shame in both parents and their children. Instead of escalating nonconstructive behaviors when experiencing disappointment, disrespect, and disconnection (all triggers of shame), family members showed higher levels of self-control and an improved ability to communicate with each other – even though they were not coached in communication strategies! Even more fascinating were my experiences with what are called "public opinion" interventions. In these interventions, the child's or adolescent's aggressive behaviors are publicized and lead to the involvement of other people from the social network. Colleagues hearing about these interventions would often protest "but you are shaming the child!" At first I didn't know how to respond to their objections. Yet now, after 15 years of practicing this type of therapy, I understand that the critics were right in addressing the presence of shame in the intervention, but had got it all wrong regarding the effects of the intervention. As a result of experiencing the interventions, the children's shame did not increase; it had actually become regulated: they became more willing to accept criticism and admit to their mistakes, they became closer to their families and were willing to do things which they had avoided earlier such as school work, household chores, and spending time with their families to name a few.

My approach to regulating shame is also inspired and deeply influenced by Dan Wile's Collaborative Couples Therapy (Wile 1993, 2008). Whereas Wile's therapeutic model addresses the entire spectrum of emotions, one can treat his books as manuals for shame regulation in working with couples. From the CCT model, I have adopted the principle that assigns great importance to fostering a collaborative attitude as the main vehicle for regulating shame reactions. I have also followed Wile's unique style of regulating communication in the therapy room and have tried to emulate his way of simultaneously addressing private, interpersonal, and systemic aspects of emotional dysregulation. I have worked intensively with the CCT model in the last 10 years and expanded it to assist children and their families. My experience has convinced me that the most efficacious format for conducting shame regulation therapy is the "triangle," that is, the presence of three people in the therapy room: therapist, parent, and child; therapist and two siblings or therapist with two parents.

## *The Structure of the Book*

The book comprises two parts. The first, "Understanding Shame," describes some of the major dynamics of shame. I do not intend this part to provide a comprehensive overview of shame experiences, as many other books have done this sufficiently. Rather, I focus on the practical aspects related to the process of shame regulation in therapy.

Chapter 1, "Opening our Eyes," describes some of the basic shame experiences in children and their families. Using the biblical story of the Garden of Eden as a background, I present an introduction to the emotion of shame, elaborating when and why people experience shame and how it affects them.

Chapter 2, "Fighting with Shame," describes the main ways in which shame influences and is influenced by relationships. In this chapter, I focus on two predominant effects of shame on relationships – attacking and withdrawing. I show how easy it is to succumb to these dynamics and suggest practical means of extricating oneself from them.

Chapter 3, "Communicating with Shame: Monitoring the Presence of Shame in Conversations," discusses how shame disrupts interpersonal communication and how it can provide clues about important (unresolved) issues in a relationship.

The Second part of the book, "Regulating Shame," details specific interventions for regulating shame in individuals, as well as within families and schools.

In Chapter 4, "Systemic Mirroring: A Model for Shame Regulation," I describe my main intervention for shame management – the Systemic Mirroring intervention.

In Chapter 5, "Regulating the Shame of Parents: Helping Them to Become the Best Team They Can Be," I present an integrated parent–couple approach aimed at transforming parental fights fueled by shame into constructive and intimate conversations, thus helping both parents to become a highly effective shame-regulating team.

Chapter 6, "Regulating Intense Shame of Non-Cooperative Adolescents: When Dialogue Breaks Down," focuses on interventions for shame management when the main shame-afflicted person is unwilling (or unable) to cooperate. In this chapter, I present interventions for dealing with the state of shamelessness.

Chapter 7, "Regulating Shame in Schools: All You Need Is Respect," is the last chapter in the book. Here I address the dynamics of shame regulation between teachers and students, and between teachers and parents in the school environment.

The basic tenet of the approach presented in this book is that shame is best regulated through specialized conversations that elicit openness, vulnerability, and ultimately intimacy. Accordingly, throughout the book, I present short verbal exchanges to model "how it is done." At the same time, I also address the limitations of regulating others' and our own shame. I believe that understanding these limitations (instead of trying to be perfect/god like) allows us to accept our and others' imperfections.

## References

Omer, H. (2004). *Non-Violent Resistance: A New Approach to Violent and Self-destructive Children*. Cambridge University Press

Wile, D. B. (1993). *After the fight: Using your disagreements to build a stronger Relationship*. Guilford Press

Wile, D. B. (2008). *After the Honeymoon: How Conflict Can Improve Your Relationship*, Revised Edition. Oakland, CA: Collaborative Couple Therapy Books

# Contents

# Chapter 1
# Opening Our Eyes

Shame is the emotion responsible for collaboration between people. In western culture, the first description of shame is found within the story of the first collaborative failure – Adam's and Eve's eating from the forbidden fruit. We usually think of shame as attached to a very specific part of the story: Adam's and Eve's realization of being exposed. However, this is only one thread in the fabric of shame revealed by this story. In this chapter, I will use this story to identify the important features associated with shame and the ways in which they play out in relationships and in the therapeutic encounter.

## 1.1 Expectations and Standards

The story begins after god has planted a garden in Eden and gives man permission to eat all the fruits of the garden, except the ones that belong to the tree of knowledge. Later, the serpent approaches the woman and suggests that she eat from the fruit of the tree. She initially refuses out of fear:

Woman: "God has said, '*You shall not* eat from it or touch it, or you will die'."

According to evolutionary psychologists, shame in its earliest forms regulated social behavior within groups of early hominids, setting boundaries for individuals who were not adhering to group norms (Fessler 2004). It is the emotion that functioned to balance self-interest and the interest of the group, and it is the feeling one would have when one did not meet group standards (Sedikides and Skowronski 1997; Gilbert 2007).

Wherever there is shame, there are standards that were not respected. Adam and Eve experience shame after they have transgressed God's standards (eating from the



U. Weinblatt, *Shame Regulation Therapy for Families*,
https://doi.org/10.1007/978-3-319-77470-1_1

forbidden tree), and while God's expectation was explicit, it is the many implicit, half-conscious expectations that make us most vulnerable to experiencing shame:

Wife: "I don't know why he has to ruin our Friday dinner every week!"
Husband: "Ruin! I was the one who cooked everything!"
Wife: "You did, but you also screamed and yelled and acted like a child!"
Husband (to therapist): "I cooked the whole day, and when they decided not to eat a thing, I blew up. What would you do have done?"

In relationships, whenever we do something for the other, we expect reciprocity. We expect the other to see, recognize, appreciate, or do something in return. If that other person fails to do so, we can experience shame. In this example, the father cooked and expected his wife and children to eat his food (and probably also expected them to enjoy it). When they didn't – he experienced intense shame that led him to explode.

Shame can be triggered by others not adhering to our expectations, yet it is more commonly triggered as a result of our failure to meet our own standards (Keltner and Buswell 1996; Deonna et al. 2012). Referring to this point, leading shame theorists (Lewis 1971) have emphasized that shame is a result of a discrepancy between what we expect from ourselves (ideal ego) and our actual performance. The higher and more rigid are our expectations – the more vulnerable we become to experiencing shame.

Vulnerability to shame leads often to an aversion to standards and expectations, for any kind of expectation can immediately lead to a strong emotional reaction:

Father (in session with his son): "We have simple expectations from our son and he never meets them!"
Son: "So don't have any expectations!"
Father (to therapist): "You see, this is what I was talking about, he only does what he wants to do and doesn't care about anybody else!"
Therapist (to father): "I think what your son was trying to tell you is, 'I don't want expectations because I am afraid that I will not meet them, and then you will be disappointed with me'."
Therapist (to son): "Is that what you meant?"
Son: "Yes, they are always disappointed with me. I can't stand it anymore."

People experiencing high levels of shame usually have a history of not meeting their own or others' expectations. They will develop a fear of disappointing themselves or others, a fear they will deal with by trying to avoid situations in which people have certain hopes for them. In some cases they even purposely fail, fearing that being successful will lead others to have expectations of them:

Therapist: "I am really impressed with how you dealt with resolving conflicts with your kids this week."
Mother (suddenly looking anxious): "It was nothing."
Therapist (smiling): "I am sorry if I now caused you to worry that I will expect you to be like that every week…"

Mother (smiling): "Yes, I don't like expectations."
Therapist (smiling): "On the other hand, I hope that you are not now planning on deliberately failing…"
Mother (smiling): "I was just starting to think about that…"

I believe that the fear of expectations is what causes certain adolescents (but also younger kids) to react negatively to positive reinforcement. For example, in a recent consultation in a school for kids with behavioral problems, the principal shared with me her new insights on relating with one of her most explosive students. This ten-year-old, who had been making progress in the previous months, would immediately regress after the principal reinforced his good behavior. "I learned that I can't show him any excitement about his improved behavior and grades. It seems that every time I wanted to show my appreciation, he would lose his focus and act out. I learned that I need to let him know that I am aware of his improvement, but not show any further anticipation or expectations. What strengthens the motivation of other students weakens this child's motivation." A recent study investigating the impact of praise on children supports this principal's observation – it seems that children with low self-esteem react negatively to being praised in an inflated way (Brummelman et al. 2014); in the study, the kids with low self-esteem that were praised more enthusiastically were the ones who would later avoid dealing with additional difficult tasks.

An issue closely related to standards and expectations is the notion of disappointment. Disappointments elicit shame, and shamed people often feel like disappointments. The fear of disappointments leads to various avoidant behaviors, distancing, and the tendency to lower expectations from ourselves and others:

Husband: "She doesn't care about me anymore!"
Wife: "He is right; I care less."
Therapist (to wife): "And do you want to care for him? If you could choose, would you choose to care?"
Wife: "I don't know, he disappointed me so many times. This way, I won't be disappointed again."

Lowering expectations is the most common reaction people have after they have experienced shame. While this mechanism does provide some protection from becoming disappointed, it also leads to caring less, becoming disconnected, and giving up hope. These are heavy prices to pay in order to avoid feeling the shame.

## 1.2 Curiosity and Joy

While Eve initially declines the serpent's suggestion to eat from the tree in fear of violating God's standard, the serpent persists, and Eve's curiosity conquers her fear. She thus "eats from it, *enjoys* the fruit and gives some to her husband."

It was initially Eve's curiosity about the fruit and her enjoyment of it that played an activating role in the story leading to the shame experience. Tomkins (1963) stressed that shame is the emotion most related to the deactivation of pleasurable activities. It is triggered when there is an abrupt change or reduction in our level of joy, and it is also the emotion that inhibits the ability to feel enjoyment, excitement, and to be curios (Nathanson 1992). Shame in its functional and constructive form supports the shift from being absorbed in pleasurable activities to facing the tasks of everyday reality.

In relation to joy and curiosity, three common behaviors are observed in individuals who have difficulties regulating their shame: difficulty in stopping pleasurable activities, difficulty in experiencing joy, and difficulty in being curious.

The difficulty in stopping pleasurable activities is of course common for all children (and for many adults) but becomes much more intense for children who experience high levels of shame. They will want to play and enjoy themselves and will not be able to stop. With such kids it seems as if they don't have enough shame – that is, the positive inhibiting component of shame which stops us from endlessly having fun is not functioning adequately. Once these children are stopped, they experience intense shame and humiliation and often do not want to continue collaborating. With older children or adolescents, a variation of this process is manifested during the therapeutic process in their will to speak only about things that bring them pleasure. Once the conversation is channeled to less enjoyable subjects, they will stop communicating. Thus, one sign that a child or an adolescent is improving in his or her ability to regulate shame is his or her cessation of pleasurable activities without exploding.

The inability to experience joy is the flip side of the difficulty of stopping joyful activities. Here, shame diminishes the motivation and the legitimacy to enjoy oneself. The prohibition to enjoy becomes even more intense in situations that involve other people:

Therapist: "How was your weekend?"
Adolescent: "Not fun."
Therapist: "What happened?"
Adolescent: "My parents forced me to go with them to the beach. They enjoyed themselves and I hated every minute."

While such behaviors are considered for adolescents common and within the normal range of shame, at other times, the shame response is so intense that events which we would expect to lead one to have joy are experienced differently:

Client: "I didn't do anything this week. I told my husband that I am not willing to go out to a restaurant, go to the beach or go to a movie. I refused to participate in anything."
Therapist: "You didn't want to go to a restaurant because…"
Client: "Because of the people. I don't want them to see me."
Therapist: "You don't want to be seen because…"
Client: "They would see how pathetic I am."
Therapist: "And if you would, for some reason, enjoy yourself there…?"
Client: "That would make me look even more ridiculous."

Related to the reduction of joy is the effect shame has on curiosity. In general, the more shame we experience in relationship to something, the faster we will lose interest in this object. In family conflicts, a common manifestation of this process occurs when one family member feels shamed and as a result quickly loses interest in what the other has to say:

Husband (to therapist): "She just looked at me with this horrible face and said 'Who do think you are?'"
Wife (tries to explain): "I just wanted to…"
Husband: "She treated me as if I were her worst enemy! No respect, no caring, no nothing!"
Wife: "What I tried to tell you is…"
Husband: "I just can't believe she treated me this way…"
Therapist: "I think your wife is trying to explain herself. Do you want to know what she is thinking?"
Husband: "No, I really don't care what she thinks!"

The loss of curiosity related to shame is one of the biggest obstacles for therapies and counseling processes which center their efforts on improving communication and problem solving. Because shame reduces people's ability to be curious and interested in hearing what the other has to say, when shame exceeds a certain threshold, the potential for a meaningful dialogue is lost. In such circumstances, counselors often ask clients to try to be curios although they can't. This unfortunately can lead clients to become even more ashamed ("I am a failure for not being able to be curious").

The relationship between shame, curiosity, and joy is extremely important in therapeutic and educational work, because curiosity and joy are some of the clearest signs that shame is being regulated (Fosha 2000). And yet, surprisingly, an exciting and joyful session can also backfire, especially for individuals who are susceptible to shame. Without preparation, such sessions can flood the person with intense pain, leaving them baffled and clueless as to what triggered this intense emotional reaction. For example, a client reported that after a joyful and exciting session, she felt lousy upon returning home:

Client: "I felt tense, as if I had done something terribly wrong."
Therapist: "What was going through your mind?"
Client: "Like I had a voice saying to me, 'Who do think you are??? You are disgusting!'"

It was as if she had eaten from a forbidden fruit and was now punished for it. Thus, while joy, excitement, and curiosity are signals that shame is regulated, they are also precarious states leaving the person exposed to experiencing shame later. Without planning for and anticipating this backlash, moments of joy can turn into nightmares.

## 1.3 Hiding, Secrecy, and Avoidance

After Adam and Eve ate the fruit, "*the eyes of both of them were opened*, and they knew that they were naked; and they sewed fig leaves together and made themselves loin coverings." Next, God enters into the story. Hearing Him walk in the garden, the man and the woman hide in the trees. God calls to the man:

God: "Where are you?"
Man: "I heard your voice in the garden and I was afraid because I was naked; so I hid."

Adam and Eve's first reaction to eating from the tree was the opening of their eyes. The eyes, as Wurmser (1981) noted, are the "organ of shame." It is the eyes of others that evoke our embarrassment and shame, and it is in the eyes of the other that we can see whether we have value. Still, the shame experience does not necessarily require the presence of other people; it happens when we evaluate ourselves, when our eyes "turn inward" (Morrison 1987). At those times, we are the ones shaming ourselves, blaming ourselves, and punishing ourselves.

Shame is the emotion most related to the self and to the question "who am I?" It is through the interacting with others that we develop identity, and it is through this interaction that we experience shame. When we experience shame, our answer to the question of "who am I?" is "I am bad," "I am a failure," or "I am weak." Since it does not make much sense to publicize such conclusions, the more shame we have, the more we feel the need to hide our true identity from the world. Actually, the word "shame" is derived from the Indo-European word "skam" or "skem," which means to hide, and it is out of these roots that we derive the word skin. It is then no wonder that we describe people who are not easily shamed as "thick skinned" and those who are vulnerable to shame as "thin skinned."

When people have done something which is shameful, they try to cover it up. After Adam and Eve ate the forbidden fruit, they became aware of their nakedness, then covered themselves with fig leaves, and hid from God. Indeed, evasion, concealment, and camouflaging are the first responses to experiencing shame. When we feel shame, we feel exposed, naked, and vulnerable; it is in such situations that hiding and protecting ourselves become the most urgent goals (Morrison 1989; Morrison 2011).

Hiding is not always a damaging reaction. Sometimes the procedure of insulating from others is part of finding a safe haven where we can recuperate and lick our own wounds while keeping the shaming provoking people in a distance. The temptation to hide and to move away from others is always something that needs to be managed, for such imposed isolation can easily deepen the hold of shame in our emotional life. In the hope of finding a haven where there is "no right and no wrong," people can find themselves reigning over kingdoms of isolation in which the most potent possibility for reducing shame – connecting to others – is neutralized.

When we feel shame, we not only wish to hide from the world, but also wish to hide from ourselves. What do we hide? Feelings, thoughts, and needs that might make us look weak, inferior, or damaged. By hiding, we become extremely selective in what we share with the world, and as shame intensifies, important information is routinely censored from others and also from ourselves. While we are more aware of making decisions to withhold or avoid sharing our information with others, we are less aware of how we become blind to our own thoughts and emotions which are shame related.

In the process of regulating shame, we typically focus and put effort in changing patterns of hiding from others and from ourselves. Let us look first at a pattern of hiding from others:

Son: "It is as if you do everything wrong!"
Mother: "I am trying, but you just pick on what is wrong; you blame me all the time."
Son: "Because you don't listen! And then when I yell, you blame me for being violent!"
Therapist (to son): "I see what you are trying to do. You want a different relationship with your mother, but the only thing that comes out is your anger. Still, I can see that you also care about your mother, although you don't let her know that; it's like you hide it."
Son: "Yes. I can't let her know that."

Shame likes to hide behind anger (Potter-Efron 2007), and there is a good reason for that. While shame makes us feel weak, anger makes us feel strong. The transformation of shame to anger is so quick that it is often missed by all the involved parties. They focus on the anger and not on the real issue – shame. Dynamics of concealment and hiding are also common in situations in which family members will not divulge aggressive, violent, or other dysfunctional behaviors manifested by another family member, to people outside of the family circle:

Mother: "My son often hits me at home."
Therapist: "Who knows about this?"
Mother: "No one. If I ever tell, he will never forgive me."
Therapist: "It is important that others know."
Mother: "Won't that stigmatize him?"

In this example, information is withheld from others to prevent the child from experiencing shame. These dynamics of secrecy have been the target of many family therapy interventions in situations of abuse in the family. These interventions are based on the assumption that breaking the seal of secrecy, that is, disclosing the shameful behaviors of family members with others is a major stepping stone in the process of emancipation from shame for the victims (Sanderson 2015) and the introduction of healthy shame to the perpetrators (Ahmed et al. 2001).

Just like hiding from others can be exhibited in numerous ways, so can withholding information from ourselves. Sometimes this process is done consciously, but it is often done outside of awareness. This process has been referred to as "the bypassing of shame" (Kaufman 1996) and describes the course in which important information becomes unavailable to us, by being split off from our awareness. These phenomena are much more common than people realize and are the main reason that, during conflict, people lose their abilities; they lose skills that are easily available to them when they are not experiencing shame.

When the process of hiding escalates, it leads to accelerated avoidance and to the splitting of information on multiple levels. Just like the anxiety-avoidant person will fear and avoid any situation that might illicit anxious feelings, the shame-avoidant person will avoid situations that might cause them to feel shame. Whether the hiding is from ourselves or from others, the consequences are often the same: we lose the connection to who we really are, we lose the ability to connect authentically and honestly with others, and we remain stuck with our shame, all alone.

## 1.4 Accusation and Blaming

An almost comic part of the story of the Garden of Eden is the way that Adam and Eve try to deal with God's accusations. What do they do? What we all do when accused – we blame others. Adam claims it was his wife's fault: "The woman *whom you gave* to be with me, she gave me from the tree, and I ate." Then God asks Eve why she ate, which leads her to blame the serpent. Each one blames another; no one accepts responsibility and admits his or her own failures.

Where there is blame, there is shame. By blaming, the shamed person is trying to transfer shame from themselves to others (Kaufman 1996; Stuewig et al. 2010). Blaming is the most common shame regulating strategy, and the more it is used, the more we can assume that this person is experiencing shame:

Mother (to son after he played with his glass of water and spilled it): "Look what you have done! You spilled it! I told you to stop playing with it!"
Son (feeling shame): "It's Sarah's fault (the sister). Why did she give me such a tall glass?"

Blame is so common that we tend to become blind to it (although we still react to it). Blame and related behaviors, such as criticism, camouflage themselves in diverse communication practices, all of which send the message, "I am good you are bad." Let us look, for example, at a heated parenting session:

Father: "You are too soft with the kids, you let them walk all over you."
Mother: "No I am not! What are you talking about?!"
Father: "I am talking about letting him watch TV the whole day!"
Mother: "And what did you do on Sunday with the kids? Do you call that quality time, watching TV from morning till evening?"
Father: "You know, it is impossible to talk to you; you never accept anything that I say!"
Mother: "That is because you never say anything nice; you just blame, blame, blame."
Father: "Now you are starting to remind me of your mother and how she treated your father."
Mother: "You are right, I am not only a bad mother but also a bad wife!"

In this escalating fight, both sides use different variations of putting blame (and shame) on the other. Whether through direct attack, denying, bringing evidence, counterattacking, interpreting, or self-accusations, the partners are focusing on the "bad" behavior of the other and are unable to share what is really bothering them.

Blame is the biggest clue that shame is present and under-regulated, and when people can admit to their faults, we know that shame has been regulated.

## 1.5 Mistakes, Betrayal, and Revenge

God's reaction to Adam and Eve's transgression is harsh. He decides to punish painfully:

(To Woman) "I will greatly multiply your pain in childbirth, in pain you will bring forth children."

(To Man) "Because you have listened to the voice of your wife, and have eaten from the tree about which I commanded you, saying, 'You shall not eat from it'; cursed is the ground because of you; in anguish you will eat of it all the days of your life."

Yet these punishments are not enough, and in the final act God sends Adam and Eve out of the garden because "he (Adam) might stretch out his hand, and take also from the tree of life."

The Garden of Eden story highlights the shame of Adam and Eve. Yet, God's revengeful behavior and the harsh punishments he inflicted on Adam, Eve, and the serpent indicate that He is also experiencing intense shame; shame derived from feeling betrayed. Betrayal and exclusion are the greatest threats to collaboration and as such, are also what triggers the most intense shame reactions. On the emotional level, revenge aims to regulate such intense shame. It is a strategy of shifting shame from one person to another, of regaining a sense of esteem and respect.

All of us experience minor betrayals on a daily basis:

Father (angry): "I told you to turn off the computer at 20:00, I can't believe you are still playing on it!"

Son: "This is really important, I'll finish in a minute."

Father: "No, finish now; I don't trust you to turn it off by yourself."

And such betrayals can also lead to minor acts of revenge:

Father: "You know what, because you didn't respect the limits I set, no computer for you till the end of the week."

Most of us will not view the son's behavior as a betrayal and the father's response as an act of revenge. Instead, we will define the child's behavior as "noncompliance" and the father's as "consequences" or as "punishment." However, on the emotional level, the father's response resembles retribution, accomplishing what revenge does – it regulates one person's shame by placing it onto another.

When people feel hurt and inferior, they can easily legitimize and even feel morally obligated to hurt back. The pain of shame demands us to do something that will counter that pain, something that will make us feel good. Recent studies mirror the complexities of taking revenge. On the one hand, some studies explain why taking revenge can be so tempting – it seems that revenge is connected with areas of the brain that positively reinforce us (De Quervain et al. 2004). Yet other studies show that contemplating revenge can make us obsessive and keep us dealing with the hurt, long after others, who solved the offense in other ways, have moved on with their lives (Carlsmith et al. 2008). Interestingly, it seems that what gives us the most satisfaction in the act of revenge is not when we cause the other to experience pain, but rather, when we cause them to understand what they did wrong and to take responsibility for their actions (Gollwitzer et al. 2011). This indicates that some acts of revenge ultimately aim to restore the ability to collaborate.

But did Adam and Eve's behavior demand such retaliation by God? Couldn't their behavior be viewed as a naïve slipup, a temporary failure of judgment, a mistake? When shame is not regulated, the answer is no. In such situations, there is no room for mistakes, no containment of the other, no forgiveness. Rather, mistakes are condemned and punished harshly. In such situations we cannot forgive others and cannot forgive ourselves. In the story, it is God who punishes man, yet when people are experiencing intense shame, they punish themselves without need of an external entity to punish them.

## 1.6 Rejection and Pain

Before God expels Adam and Eve from the garden, he punishes them harshly. The storyteller emphasizes the pain involved in these punishments, and indeed, shame, rejection, and pain are highly connected (MacDonald and Leary 2005). Most words that describe social rejection are typically reserved for physical pain, and neural studies have shown that the same regions, which process physical pain, also process the pain of social rejection and exclusion (Eisenberger et al. 2003).

People experiencing shame often complain of pain, pain so great that it demands extreme counteractions to sooth it. In the last decade, a pain/shame soothing practice that became common among adolescents and young adults is cutting themselves. In an attempt to escape the pain which is associated with triggers described in this chapter – disappointments, failures, rejection, self-blame, and self-hatred – these young people develop pain-regulating rituals that shift their attention from the shame-induced pain to the act of self-injury.

While cutting is a new strategy for regulating shame, rejection and exclusion have a very long tradition. In the final act of the story, God sends Adam and Eve out of the garden. This is exactly what shame ultimately leads to: being rejected or rejecting the person who shamed us. When we are shamed, we often do not want to ever again see the person who hurt us so:

Wife: "I can't stay with my husband, I have to divorce him."
Therapist: "But the two of you have been doing much better."

Wife: "I know. Still I can't forget how he betrayed me. Seeing him is too painful. He needs to leave my life."

Often, during escalating interpersonal conflicts, shame becomes so intolerable that people will either threaten separation or will storm out of the room, feeling that staying would be too painful. Excluding and rejecting the shame-triggering person from our lives is a tempting solution which people usually fantasize about.

Father (after fight with daughter): "I want her out of the house!"
Mother: "But she is our daughter!"
Father: "I can no longer live with how she is treating me. We need to find a boarding school for her!"

People who experience high levels of shame usually have histories of being excluded or of excluding others:

Adolescent: "I don't have any good friends."
Therapist: "How come?"
Adolescent: "Don't know, just don't."
Therapist: "Have you ever been betrayed by a friend?"
Adolescent: "Yah, by many."
Therapist: "It's hard to trust?"
Adolescent: "Why should you trust when, in the end, they will only let you down?"

For shame-prone individuals, rejection, distancing, and even abandonment are familiar experiences which they fear and expect at the same time. They are ever vigilant to any sign of rejection and will often misread relatively neutral communications as messages of rejection:

Client: "I know you want to get rid of me!"
Therapist: "Why are you saying that?"
Client: "Because I am a burden, and I am not getting any better, and you said it yourself."
Therapist: "What did I say?"
Client: "Last time you said that you expect me to feel better soon. I thought that meant that you expect therapy to end."

In the process of shame regulation, we must always be cognizant of the danger and the capacity of intense shame to destroy relationships. When shame is unbearable, the only way to reduce shame is by having the shaming person disappear from one's life. And although such solutions can bring an end to the misery of experiencing the pain of shame, they also usually mean that we lose the ability to ever love this person again.

## References

Ahmed, E., Harris, N., Braithwaite, J., & Braithwaite, V. (2001). *Shame management through reintegration*. Melbourne: Cambridge University Press.

Brummelman, E., Thomaes, S., Overbeek, G., Orobio de Castro, B., Van Den Hout, M. A., & Bushman, B. J. (2014). On feeding those hungry for praise: Person praise backfires in children with low self-esteem. *Journal of Experimental Psychology: General, 143*(1), 9.

Carlsmith, K. M., Wilson, T. D., & Gilbert, D. T. (2008). The paradoxical consequences of revenge. *Journal of Personality and Social Psychology, 95*(6), 1316.

De Quervain, D. J., Fischbacher, U., Treyer, V., & Schellhammer, M. (2004). The neural basis of altruistic punishment. *Science, 305*(5688), 1254.

Deonna, J. A., Rodogno, R., & Teroni, F. (2012). *In defense of shame: The faces of an emotion*. New York: Oxford University Press.

Eisenberger, N. I., Lieberman, M. D., & Williams, K. D. (2003). Does rejection hurt? An fMRI study of social exclusion. *Science, 302*(5643), 290–292.

Fessler, D. M. (2004). Shame in two cultures: Implications for evolutionary approaches. *Journal of Cognition and Culture, 4*(2), 207–262.

Fosha, D. (2000). *The transforming power of affect: A model for accelerated change*. New York: Basic Books.

Gilbert, P. (2007). The evolution of shame as a marker for relationship security: A biopsychosocial approach. In J. L. Tracy, R. W. Robins, & J. P. Tangney (Eds.), *The self-conscious emotions: Theory and research* (pp. 283–309). New York: Guilford Press.

Gollwitzer, M., Meder, M., & Schmitt, M. (2011). What gives victims satisfaction when they seek revenge? *European Journal of Social Psychology, 41*(3), 364–374.

Kaufman, G. (1996). *The psychology of shame: Theory and treatment of shame-based syndrome* (2nd ed.). New York: Springer.

Keltner, D., & Buswell, B. N. (1996). Evidence for the distinctness of embarrassment, shame, and guilt: A study of recalled antecedents and facial expressions of emotion. *Cognition & Emotion, 10*(2), 155–172.

Lewis, H. B. (1971). Shame and guilt in neurosis. *Psychoanalytic Review, 58*(3), 419–438.

MacDonald, G., & Leary, M. R. (2005). Why does social exclusion hurt? The relationship between social and physical pain. *Psychological Bulletin, 131*(2), 202.

Morrison, A. P. (1987). The eye turned inward: Shame and the self. In D. L. Nathanson (Ed.), *The many faces of shame* (pp. 271–291). New York: Guilford Press.

Morrison, A. (1989). *The psychodynamics of shame. The underside of narcissism*. Hillsdale, NJ: Analytic Press.

Morrison, A. P. (2011). The psychodynamics of shame. In R. L. Dearing & J. P. Tangney (Eds.), *Shame in the therapy hour* (pp. 23–44). Washington, DC: American Psychological Association.

Nathanson, D. L. (1992). *Shame and pride: Affect, sex, and the birth of the self*. New York: WW Norton & Company.

Potter-Efron, R. (2007). *Rage: A step-by-step guide to overcoming explosive anger*. Oakland, CA: New Harbinger Publications.

Sanderson, C. (2015). *Counselling skills for working with shame*. London: Jessica Kingsley Publishers.

Sedikides, C., & Skowronski, J. J. (1997). The symbolic self in evolutionary context. *Personality and Social Psychology Review, 1*, 80–102.

Stuewig, J., Tangney, J. P., Heigel, C., Harty, L., & McCloskey, L. (2010). Shaming, blaming, and maiming: Functional links among the moral emotions, externalization of blame, and aggression. *Journal of Research in Personality, 44*(1), 91–102.

Tomkins, S. (1963). *Affect/imagery/consciousness, The negative affects* (Vol. 2). Oxford: England Springer.

Wurmser, L. (1981). *The mask of shame*. Baltimore: Johns Hopkins University Press.

# Chapter 2
# Fighting with Shame

Everyone experiences much more shame than they realize:

Wife: "Honey, did you bring the milk I asked you to get on your way home?"
Husband: "Oh shit, I forgot...."
Wife: "I can't believe this, I told you three times!"
Husband: "Well, maybe next time you should get it yourself!"

In this situation, both the wife and the husband are experiencing shame. The wife is feeling unappreciated as a result of her husband having forgotten her request. The husband is feeling like a failure. Let us look at another example:

Mother: "Michael, did you finish your homework?"
Michael: "I told you, I'll finish it in a moment."
Mother: "You said that half an hour ago. Please go and do your homework!"
Michael: "Give me just a couple more minutes; I am finishing a really important part of my computer game."
Mother: "No, please go and finish it now."
Michael: "You never let me do anything fun!"
Mother: "Stop it!"
Michael: "No, You stop it!"

Again, both sides were experiencing shame. The mother felt disrespected because she had repeatedly asked her son to do his homework, and he hadn't done it. The son, Michael, felt shamed by receiving a command from his mother. As with the former example, both sides were unaware of experiencing shame, and if they had been aware of their own shame, it would probably have made things worse. The two examples also demonstrate that most of the shame experienced is triggered unintentionally, that is – nobody, at least in the beginning of the interaction, deliberately wants to shame the other. Yet, once shame has been activated, it can easily lead to intentional shaming acts.


U. Weinblatt, *Shame Regulation Therapy for Families*,
https://doi.org/10.1007/978-3-319-77470-1_2

When people experience shame, they do one of two things: they either fight or withdraw. When fighting, conflict participants (partners, parents and children, teachers and students, etc.) try to reduce their shame by transferring it to their adversary. In withdrawing, they try to reduce their shame by hiding it. Both shame-reducing strategies have advantages and disadvantages. Fighting's big advantage is that it exposes one's shame, and, although it does not at first glance seem that way, it is an effort to communicate shame. Fighting's big disadvantage is that it evokes the other person's shame. That person will sooner or later retaliate, thus leading to more shame in the system. Withdrawal's big advantage relates to fighting's disadvantage – it keeps only one person experiencing shame. People who refrain from evoking the other's shame (whether because they care for the other or are afraid of them) will choose to withdraw, hoping that time and their own resources will be enough to manage their own shame. The disadvantage is that shame remains hidden, corroding the relationship slowly but efficiently.

## 2.1 The Dark Matter of Relationships

All of us feel shame on a daily basis, but we often don't know that we are experiencing it. It is the dark matter in relationships, an invisible driving force regulating status and intimacy. Shame is the most vital emotion in relationships. It is the level of shame that determines our ability to be open with others, consult with and get help from others, be intimate, converse and communicate, care and be cared for, and feel that we are not alone, yet awareness of it remains elusive. In our daily lives, we tend to refer much more easily to feelings such as anger, anxiety, or sadness. We more often hear people say "I feel angry", or "I feel afraid" or "I am sad," than "I feel shame." This is not surprising, as shame is the most hidden of emotions and is often expressed after it was transformed into another emotion (Lewis 1992). Clients in therapy rarely complain about feeling shame as the presenting problem (DeYoung 2015) and are, instead, in touch with more accessible emotions. However, in the growing professional literature on emotions, shame is increasingly treated as a "master emotion" in regulating relationships. It is argued that shame is evoked when relationships are disrupted, becoming either too enmeshed or too distant (Scheff 1997), and that shame is the emotion one feels when one experiences being powerless, belittled, inadequate, and disrespected (Greenberg and Goldman 2008).

## 2.2 Knowing and Not Knowing

Shame is the emotional response which delivers needed information about status within relationships. While sharing this emotional ability with other primates, we assume that only humans have been blessed (or cursed) with the additional mechanism of self awareness. This complicates the process of discovering the answer to the questions “do I have value?” and “am I important to others?” Both, our relationships to ourselves and our relationships with others, become much more complex.

Shame is a member of the family of emotions (including guilt, embarrassment, and pride) which are considered “self-conscious” (Tracy et al. 2007). This means that when shame is evoked so are processes of self-evaluation and self-reflection. When we experience shame, we judge our behavior, or who we are as a person, to be negative. Being a self-conscious emotion, we would expect to be much more aware of it, to be able to easily recognize that we have this feeling. Yet, more often than not, shame manages to escape our awareness and our knowing:

Mother: “Please clean up your room.”
Daughter: “Later.”
Mother: “Do it know!”
Daughter: “I said later. Why do you always have to nag?!”

From the outside, this interaction can be viewed as a power struggle, typifying many fights between parents and teenagers. And while a power struggle does exist, there is much more emotional involvement in the struggle than we realize. To uncover the emotions that are operating at any given moment, we need to look more closely at the unconscious inner conversation that each participant is having. Mother, for example, is having the following conversation with herself:

- “She’s irresponsible!”
- “More than that, she doesn’t care about what I say!”
- “She doesn’t respect me. If she did, she would not make such a big deal out of it.”
- “I do so much for her, and she doesn’t give anything in return.”
- “She needs to be better educated.”
- “But that is my job. She is behaving like that because I failed! I am not a good mother!”

We can easily notice that many of the thoughts reveal the presence of shame – feeling unappreciated, having no value in the eyes of others, and having no value in one’s own eyes.

Now let’s look at what is going on in the daughter’s mind:

- “She always picks on me!”
- “That is because she doesn’t like me.”
- “It is more than that, she hates me!”
- “I wish she would disappear from my life. Yes, that would be best because I’d no longer be subjected to constant messages that I am a bad daughter, irresponsible human being, a piece of shit! Yah, that is how she thinks of me! I need to let her know that I won’t *ever* let her treat me this way!”

Just like the mother is not completely aware of the shame-inducing thoughts she is having, the daughter, although immersed in these thoughts, is similarly unaware of having them. This is one of the unique features of shame – knowing and not knowing at the same time.

## 2.3 Not Wanting to Admit We Are Feeling Shame

None of us like knowing what we already know, especially when what we already know is that we are bad and weak or that we have failed. We rebel against this knowing because it feels like it won't lead to anything good. Knowing reminds us of pain which we managed to forget:

Father: "Can we talk about the low grades you have been receiving lately?"
Daughter: "Can we not talk about it?"
Father: "We really need to talk about it."
Daughter: "No, *you* need to talk about it; I don't."
Father (angry): "You see, this is your problem. *you* always…."

Therapist (interrupting father): "I think that what your daughter is trying to tell you is, 'I don't think that talking about the grades will do any good. Actually, I fear that talking about it will make me feel even worse. I know what I need to do.' (To daughter) Is that how you feel?"

Daughter: "Yes, that is exactly how I feel! But he doesn't understand."
Father: "So, what is the solution? To not talk, to close our eyes?!"

Surprisingly, the more shame we experience, the less we are inclined to admit it – both to ourselves and to others. It is as if the knowing weakens us and threatens to increase the shame reaction. It is as if the admitting to experiencing shame exposes us further, when what we need is to be covered and protected.

"Refusing to take responsibility," "always denying," "not caring," and "not cooperating" are common accusations of people who are in a relationship with someone who is experiencing high levels of shame. The inability to admit and accept the experience of shame damages the ability to collaborate, problem solve, and have meaningful dialogue. It leads to interactions in which people either withdraw (don't put issues that bother them "on the table" (out of fear of the other's dismissal)) or fight (try to push an endless variety of agendas, which receive only a stubborn, non-cooperative stance from the other).

Admitting to having shame and admitting that we inflicted shame on the other are the means to transcend fighting and withdrawing. As we discussed, this demands (a) knowing that we are experiencing shame and (b) wanting to admit that we are experiencing it. At first glance, these obstacles might seem as if they are not that difficult to overcome, but when a person is experiencing intense shame, they become tough barriers. The strength of the feeling, itself, obscures our knowledge that we are actually experiencing shame, and it diminishes the will to cooperate and collaborate. In such moments, people will not admit their shame, even when they know that it is helpful, and, instead, shift to the less effective strategies of fighting or withdrawing.

## 2.4 Not Knowing How to Talk When We Feel Shame

Even when we want to share our shame, we often get stuck in not knowing how to communicate our feelings to the other. Indeed, while most of us cannot recognize that we are experiencing shame, we can identify feeling hurt, angry, or distressed. Feeling like that, we try to communicate what is happening to us. However, when shame exceeds a certain level, talking can become dangerous and lead to more shame:

Husband: "I really didn't like how you behaved in my parent's house this evening."
Wife: "What exactly didn't you like?"
Husband: "You didn't eat anything, and everybody noticed it."
Wife: "I told you a thousand times that I don't like your mother's cooking. Why can't we just go out?"

The husband in this example felt shame about his wife's behavior. He thought that his parents viewed his wife's behavior negatively and, as a result, view him negatively. He attempts to talk with his wife about it, and the conversation deteriorates quickly. She feels blamed, unappreciated, and shamed by what he says, and she responds in ways that lead him to experience more shame.

Let's look at another example:

Mother: "I want to talk with you about how you behaved towards me when we went shopping."
Daughter: "O.k. talk, it's a free country."
Mother: "I felt that you were really rude to me."
Daughter: "Not agreeing with everything you say makes me rude???"
Mother: "No, but publicly screaming at me that you hate a shirt which I offered you does fit the definition of being rude."
Daughter: "I told you five times that I don't like that shirt, and you kept on insisting. I really hate going shopping with you."
Mother: "I think you just suggested a great solution; we will stop going shopping!"
Daughter: "Are you threatening me now? Cause it's really not working!"

The mother tries to communicate the shame she felt about her daughter's behavior toward her in the shopping mall, yet the conversation quickly escalates. This happens as a result of the daughter becoming shamed by what her mother is saying. What she hears is, "You are a rude person." This leaves the mother and daughter in a shame loop in which each side's effort to communicate shame just increases the other person's shame.

Since many of us experience variations of such dialogues in our relationships, we frequently think hard before we raise an issue with someone who is close to us. We hope that time will solve the problem and that we will forget what got us upset, cool down, or find something else to distract us – open our computer, watch TV, or talk with a friend. And such solutions sometimes do work, and we really manage to let go. Yet, the stronger the shame we experience, the more difficult it is to move on. When it comes to shame, time is not always an effective natural healer. We can carry feelings of hurt, humiliation, and insignificance for a long time, and when we decide to keep silent rather than communicating these feelings, they can turn into resentment, distancing, and may ultimately lead to the destruction of the relationship.

## 2.5 Talking While Being Aware of Shame

There are different ways of talking, and they differ in their goals. When talking is employed to solve a problem, we risk increasing the shame in the system. Let's look again at the two examples. In both situations, the speaker tried to solve a problem: the husband tried to collaborate with his wife in finding a way for her to behave differently when they visit his parents; and the mother tried to find a way to get her daughter to refrain from yelling at her when they go shopping. The husband and the mother also intended to communicate feelings –the husband said "I didn't like…" and the mother said "I felt you were rude to me." Yet both of them (somewhat unconsciously) sent the same message: "You were wrong." This message is exactly the one that evokes shame and causes the listeners to retaliate.

From a shame regulation perspective, the main challenge in a given conversation is figuring out how to express our shame without shaming the other.

Let's look at how the husband and the mother could have done it differently:

Husband: "I am feeling pretty lousy."
Wife: "Why?"
Husband: "I want to share this with you, but don't want you to feel like I am criticizing you."
Wife: "Just say it."
Husband: "It sounds silly, but I'm wondering why you didn't eat anything at my parents' house."
Wife: "I told you a thousand times, I don't like your mother's cooking! Why can't we just go out? Your family is so cheap!"
Husband: "I know you hate her cooking; you know that I hate it too. I'm just saying that it makes me uncomfortable when you refuse to eat there."
Wife: "You want me to force myself to eat?"
Husband: "No, I am not blaming you. I am just saying that the situation stinks and leaves me feeling bad."
Wife: "Well, if you really want to know, I feel bad too. It's not the best situation for me either. I don't like the looks your mother shoots me, and this time I actually tried to swallow some of her undercooked quiche. I can still taste the raw eggs…."
Husband (smiling): "I guess I got used to it, eating it for so long…."
Wife (smiling): "And your father has eaten it for so long that he actually likes it."
Husband (smiling): "Watch out, that might happen to you…."

Did the husband solve the problem of his wife not eating at his parents' house? No, but he moved in the right direction. That is to say, he moved in the direction of reducing both his wife's and his own shame. The husband in this conversation is taking a different approach from how most people communicate. He is doing what Dan Wile (2002) calls "solving the moment," that is, he is trying to express his discomfort and his shame while remaining sensitive to avoid shaming his wife. This is a dramatic shift from conversations that focus on "solving the problem." The husband is sensitive to his wife's shame, because he knows that if her shame reaches a certain threshold, the ability to communicate effectively will end.

Let us now look at how the mother could have spoken differently with her daughter:

Mother: "You know, I am still thinking about our shopping trip."
Daughter: "What??"
Mother: "It didn't work out so well."
Daughter: "I know! Why does it always have to be this way with you."
Mother: "Yes, this happens to us a lot."
Daughter: "If you would just let me choose, none of this would happen."
Mother: "You are probably right, but I have opinions too."
Daughter: "I know you have opinions, but I really liked the other shirt."
Mother: "It's a shame that we don't have the same taste in clothes."
Daughter: "Yah, you want to dress me like someone old, like someone who's thirty or forty years old!"
Mother: "Yah, and you want to dress like you are 20, when you're only 13."
Daughter: "All of my friends dress that way…."
Mother: "Well, they are not my daughters. I care about you."
Daughter (hesitating and then smiling): "You are lucky, Anna would have yelled at you much louder. Did you see how she treated her mom when we had the parent-teacher conference?"
Mother (smiling): "Yah, that was bad…."
Daughter (smiling): "You are lucky you have a daughter like me!"

The mother in this conversation is trying to do the same thing the husband was doing in the former interaction – to uncover her own shame, while not shaming her daughter. We can see that this is not simple and that the mother bypasses a few crossroads where she could have entered into a fight with the daughter. She manages not to fall into these traps, because her shame is regulated. The mother, just like the husband in the previous dialogue, did not solve the problem of finding a way to go shopping without fighting. The mother and daughter did not reach an agreement, nobody explicitly apologized, and there are no new plans for the future. Yet, the conversation managed to regulate the shame which was produced in the conflict, by helping the participants admit to their roles, move closer to each other, and, together, view the problem from a higher perspective. Such conversations also have an immunizing effect. The next time they find themselves in the same situation, they will experience it a little bit differently and be just a little bit more protected from experiencing shame.

## 2.6 Withdrawing

When shame is present and there is no fighting, there is withdrawing: remaining silent, watching too much TV, working longer hours, playing on the computer, binge eating, alcohol, drugs, fantasizing, and sleeping – the means for withdrawal are endless. That is what makes the avoidant, silent, and distancing reactions of shame so difficult to work with – they are hard to detect.

The group of behaviors that we categorize as withdrawal reflect shame's other symptomatic expression, the tendency to escape and hide (Schoenleber and Berenbaum 2012). As we have mentioned in Chap. 1, this hiding is directed toward others and toward ourselves. When we hide from others, we experience shame but do not let others know it:

Wife: "You seem distant, is everything o.k.?"
Husband: "Yes."
Wife: "Are you sure? You don't look that way."
Husband: "Yes I am sure, really, everything is fine."
Wife: "Did I do anything that hurt you?"
Husband: "No, can you let it go?"

Being exposed as weak or as having failed activates, the function of the self is to cover and protect itself when it is exposed unwillingly. In such states, the idea of revealing shame feels counterproductive and irrational. It resembles demanding that a depressed person be happy or that an angry person calm down. Yet, in relationships we expect such openness and are frustrated when the other will not share how they feel with us. Moreover, we interpret withdrawal as a part of a power struggle, as an act of resistance. Of course, withdrawal behaviors can be part of a power struggle, as shown in the case of "the silent treatment," but in such cases, we are really dealing with a type of fight and its logic (transferring shame to the other), and not the psychology of true withdrawal.

Withdrawing is often experienced by the other as a refusal to cooperate:

Therapist: "So tell me. why are you here?"
Mother (to son): "Why are we here?"
Son: "Don't know."
Mother: "You don't know?!"
Son: "Yes, I don't know."
Mother: "Well, we are here because we fight almost every day, and yesterday my son even pushed me. Now do you know why we are here?"
Son: "Whatever."

Non-collaborative states almost always reflect the presence of shame and are the result of dynamics we discussed earlier in this chapter:

- The inability to know what one is feeling
- The inability to admit what one is feeling
- The lack of will to reveal and expose
- The inability to communicate even when the will is present

These four factors constitute the "loss of voice" which means the inability to communicate the experience of shame, which will be described in more detail in Chap. 4.

Hiding from others composes only the first type of withdrawal behavior; the second type is composed of hiding from the self. It is what Nathanson (1992) referred to in his "compass of shame" as "avoidance" – behaviors intended to help us shift our attention away from shame, get it out of our awareness, and diminish its existence. On one level or another, all of us use this strategy on a daily basis. Instead of experiencing a feeling that makes us feel bad about ourselves, we find ourselves checking the smartphone, writing a text message, watching a football game, or going to sleep – any activity meant to distract us from the uncomfortable feeling.

As shame intensifies, the imperative to stop feeling it becomes urgent as a result of it being such a painful sensation. Thus, just as physically pain-packed experiences demand that one dissociates from the pain in order to survive, the same holds true for the emotionally pain-packed experience of shame. In situations of this kind, people try to block the pain of shame by numbing themselves through different pain relieving self-medications. In addition, natural numbing psychological mechanisms become active:

Client: "I am talking to you, but I can't feel anything."
Therapist: "What is this like for you?"
Client: "It makes everything meaningless, boring, and without value."
Therapist: "I remember that in our last session you experienced a lot of pain. Could it be that part of you is protecting yourself against this pain?"
Client: "Yes, this is usually what happens; after I experience the pain, I don't feel anything for a long time."

Understanding avoidance as a pain regulation technique helps in developing a more empathetic approach toward shamed people who exhibit behaviors that usually arouse helplessness and hostility in those who care for the shamed person. However, empathy in and of itself will not always be enough to resolve intense withdrawal/avoidance behaviors. In such circumstances, an active intervention is needed to melt the barriers erected by prolonged hiding and isolation.

## 2.7 Transferring Shame

We usually don't view fighting as a way to resolve shame. Yet from an emotion regulation perspective, behaviors we typically associate with interpersonal conflict – criticism, contempt, rage, not listening, silencing, wanting to be right, etc. – are all methods of making us feel less shame as a result of seeing the other, usually the person who evoked our shame, experience a shame reaction themselves. Fighting is the means for this process of transferring shame from one person to another.

In many traditional societies, shame is transferred down the hierarchy, with the person of higher rank shaming the person of lower rank. While this still holds true in many work-related environments, it is not the way that transference of shame plays out in many contemporary family settings, where shame, blind to whom holds what position, can spread in all directions. Let's look, for example, at the following stream of events occurring in a family:

Mother (to son): "Clean up your room! Why do I always have to tell you this a thousand times?"
Son (to mother): "My room is none of your business!"
Mother (to son): "It is my business when the smell is affecting the whole house; this place is disgusting."
Son (ignores mother)
Mother: "Did you hear what I said?!"
Son (continues to ignore)
(Mother leaves the room and sees father coming in after a long day at work)
Father (to mother): "Why do I always have to come home to screaming?"
Mother (to father): "Because I do everything around the house, and you do nothing!"
Father (to mother): "Working ten hours a day is nothing?"
Mother (to father): "What do you want, a medal for providing for your family?"
(Father goes to his office and finds his daughter playing on his computer)
Father (to daughter): "I told you a thousand times that you may not play on my computer without my permission. Don't ever touch it again. I can't trust you; now get out!"
Daughter (to father): "Why do you always have to scream at me? Why can't you be like Maya's father? He is always nice to her!"
(Overhearing the conversation Grandmother comes in and says to father)
Grandmother (to father): "You were a little tough on her there; she had just started playing two minutes before you came in."
Father (to his mother): "I am not a child any more. Please, I didn't ask you to give me grades on my parenting!"

This extreme example shows how shame can be transferred from parent to child, from child to parent, from husband to wife, brother to sister, and so forth. In the example, the mother felt shame because her son hadn't cleaned his room (She had requested many times that he do so. His ongoing refusal had diminished her and left her feeling unworthy.); the son felt shamed by the parental demand and later by the criticism of his room; the mother was ashamed again when her husband complained about the house being noisy; the father was ashamed when his wife criticized him for not working more in the house and when she ridiculed him ("Do you want a medal?"); the daughter was shamed by her father, and the father was shamed back, both, by his daughter and by his mother, leading to another retaliation by him. In this example of multiple fights, shame is repeatedly transferred like a hot potato, from one family member to another, leading to multiple shame-inducing interactions.

Of course the participants are not aware of transferring the shame and don't intend to do so. If asked about the reasons for their behavior, they would talk about solving problems (son's room needing to be cleaned, stopping mother from nagging, stopping the yelling in the house, stopping the daughter from playing on the computer, etc.). While these explanations are valid and part of the picture, they also reflect the hidden ways in which shame influences motivation.

Transferring one's shame to another is often done without awareness. Fights don't usually start with the intention of having a fight but rather as an effort to improve a relationship or another's performance. Unfortunately, it is very difficult to express the desire for someone else to advance, develop, and grow, without evoking their shame. Wanting the other to improve can sound to them as if you mean that who they are right now is not good enough. This lack of awareness is also a consequence of how shame manipulates our attention, making us hyper aware of our own pain and becoming blind to the shame of the other. This selectivity in awareness leads to:

- Viewing ourselves as victims.
- Viewing the other person as the one doing the fighting. We, on the other hand, are just trying to explain, clarify, improve, or help the other to understand.
- Becoming more accusatory than we realize.

When fights escalate, the intention to shame the other (to transfer shame to the other) becomes more intentional and conscious. Alon and Omer (2006) have described the demonization processes that are part of such escalations and which lead to the imperative to degrade the other and to seek submission as the only way to resolve conflict. In such processes, shaming the other is part of a complex progression of activities that erode the other's human qualities. In situations like these, witnessing the other's shame response is not enough to make one's own shame soften up:

Father: "I am really angry at you for what you have done! You really disappointed me."
Son: "I am sorry."
Father: "That is not good enough. You did something really bad."
Son "I will try to make it better."
Father: "I just can't believe you did that. How dare you?! How dare you?!"

It is typical that in such situations, the other's shame, that is, the other person's behaviors which indicate that shame has been effectively transferred, will not be enough to extinguish the shame of the person who was originally hurt. Such behaviors are experienced as "too little too late" and can even induce more shame ("why did I have to wait so long for his apology!," "why did I have to suffer so much before he took responsibility for his actions!"). In situations of this kind, the potential for interpersonal shame management breaks down because shame is maintained by the person's inability to forgive himself for being weak, showing vulnerability, and being diminished in some way. No punishment of the other, no degradation or submission on their part, is enough to erase the feelings of humiliation that are continuously being fueled by one's own self-hatred.

## 2.8 Dangerous but Not All Bad

Fighting greatly sensitizes people to shame. For example, let us imagine that a parent and a child had a fight, and an hour later, the child asks the parent:

"Can I have a glass of water?"

Requests in general can evoke shame, for they demand that one person accept the other person's wishes and needs as momentarily outranking one's own. Yet, such a request would not elicit any significant emotional reaction from the parent had they not fought earlier, maybe just a verbal reaction such as "can you say please?" In sharp contrast, the same request after a fight can easily trigger a wave of shame-related thoughts such as:

- "What nerve to ask for something from me after the way he behaved!"
- "Does he think I am such a doormat that I will comply with his needs?"
- "He always wants and never gives!"
- "This behavior is a consequence of me being a weak parent. I need to let him know that I will not let him treat me this way!"

These thoughts might lead the parent to answer with:

"Take it yourself. I am not your slave!,"

a statement that can easily lead to another round of hostility and attacks. Fighting not only causes people to become more vulnerable to experiencing shame, it also generates more shame in the relationship; thus, the initial shame (i.e., the hurt, disrespect, humiliation, lack of appreciation) that triggered the fight is fueled by additional shame experiences, such as:

- The shame of having the fight – that is, of needing to fight in order to resolve the issue
- The shame related to how one is behaving during the fight
- The shame that is evoked by how and what the other person is doing and saying during the fight

These sources of shame are what cause fights to escalate and what make fighting such a dangerous, and often non-constructive, shame regulation strategy.

Yet fighting is important in being one of the chief means for unmasking our shame. It is by fighting that we (and the person with whom we are fighting) can uncover and discover that we are experiencing shame – that we are hurt, feel unappreciated, and are in pain. Fighting, then, is a clue that shame is present and unregulated.

Often, fights can become a prelude to an important conversation. It is through conversations and honest communication that people ultimately reduce their shame, but sometimes such conversations can occur only after a fight has erupted. Although not the optimal invitation to converse, fights often do create the conditions for important messages to be communicated, for long-held resentments to be aired, and for reciprocal reconciliation gestures to be exchanged.

Finally, fighting is sometimes the only alternative to withdrawing. Especially with people who tend to deal with their shame by avoiding, withdrawing into themselves, remaining silent, and becoming resentful. In such cases, fighting is a welcomed solution which allows more opportunities for emotional regulation:

Client: "I feel like fighting with you; I want to attack you."
Therapist: "Why is that?"
Client: "I think that the only way I will be able to connect with how I felt during the week is through fighting."
Therapist: "And what will happen if you don't attack me?"
Client: "Then I will be disconnected. Our session will be just a waste of time."

When successful, fighting helps the person who originally experienced shame to soften up. The display of shame by the other communicates understanding and the taking of responsibility and regret. It is a sign that justice has been done and that trust can be rebuilt. Such outcomes are the result of constructive fights – interactions in which there is usually mutual transferring of shame and mutual recognition by the other that shame has been transferred successfully. As both sides admit to their contribution to the problem, reveal their own hurt and vulnerability that triggered their hostile behaviors, and acknowledge how they hurt the other – the fight can transform into a moment of intimacy and healing.

## 2.9 The Shift from Hell to Heaven Is Sometimes Only One Sentence Away

We hate the people who make us experience shame and love the people who take away our shame. Often these feelings are directed toward the same person:

Husband (shouting): "I didn't like how you sided with our daughter when I criticized her; you never back me up!"
Wife: "I didn't mean to be unsupportive. I thought you were losing control. I am sorry if you felt unsupported."
Husband: "Not 'if' I felt unsupported! I hate it when you say that! You would feel the same way if you were in my situation!"
Wife: "You are right. I handled it poorly."
Husband: "Why do you always have to be that way?"
Wife: "Our daughter is really my weak spot. I don't know why I feel the need to protect her. Now that I'm thinking about it, I would do things differently if I had a second chance."
Husband: "I know she triggers you that way, but it is frustrating for me, and I fear that it is hurting my relationship with her."
Wife: "I am sorry. I will try to do better next time. You really are doing the more difficult part of the parenting."
Husband (hesitating): "Well, I am sorry too; I shouldn't have yelled at you."

Wife (reacting to the husband softening): "It's o.k., even when you shout you are still cute…."

Husband (smiling): "Our daughter knows how to press your buttons, and you know how to press mine…."

The ability of words to transform intense shame reactions is under-acknowledged. Sometimes these transformations happen as if by magic. People who experience intense shame also know, on some level, that this potential exists. That is the reason why they pressure the other to attempt to mitigate their shame, and the reason they are so frustrated when they hear non-validating or accusative statements instead of healing words.

Just as the transition from regulation to dysregulation can occur within seconds, so can the opposite movement – from feeling extreme shame to feeling no pain and beyond that to feeling an intimate moment. In the previous example, the ability of the wife to avoid becoming overly shamed by her husband's words and her ability to admit to her weakness and to the ways in which she harmed him lead to a rapid regulation of his shame response. What started as a nasty fight became a moment of connection.

Sometimes people do say the right words, words that could potentially lead to a marked reduction in the shame of the other but do it too late:

Husband (after half a year of therapy, he is suddenly saying what his wife has been wanting to hear for years): "I love you."

Wife (with a somber voice): "Good."

Which immediately shifts the husband to a shamed position:

Husband (to therapist with anger): "You see, she is never satisfied!"

What could have been a magical moment is turning more sour by the second, so the therapist quickly intervenes:

Therapist (to wife): "I thought that behind that 'good' was more. May I voice it for you?"

Wife: "Okay."

Therapist (to husband): Okay, what I thought your wife meant when she said "good" is "Don't get me wrong. I am happy that you managed to say these words to me. This is very good. At the same time, it is hard for me to celebrate it because what I am thinking to myself is, 'why did it take him so long?'" (To wife) "Is this how you feel?"

Wife: "Yes. Now that I know that he can say it, I am thinking, 'Why couldn't he say it for years? Why did I have to suffer for so long?'"

Sometimes the right words, when they are heard too late, activate a shame reaction which needs to be managed. Determination, courage, and the will to remain vulnerable is crucial:

Husband (regaining his original position after the therapist's intervention): "You are right, I really can't explain why it took so long to say it. I hope you won't be angry with me for too long."

Wife (softening and smiling): "Let start by you telling me every day that you love me, and then in a couple of months we can talk about whether I forgive you or not."

Husband (smiling to therapist): "Do you see what I have to deal with?"

## References

Alon, N., & Omer, H. (2006). *The psychology of demonization: Promoting acceptance and reducing conflict*. London: Routledge.

DeYoung, P. A. (2015). *Understanding and treating chronic shame: A relational/neurobiological approach*. New York: Routledge.

Greenberg, L. S., & Goldman, R. N. (2008). *Emotion-focused couples therapy: The dynamics of emotion, love, and power*. Washington, DC: American Psychological Association.

Lewis, M. (1992). *Shame, the exposed self*. New York: The Free Press.

Nathanson, D. L. (1992). *Shame and pride: Affect, sex, and the birth of the self*. New York: WW Norton & Company.

Schoenleber, M., & Berenbaum, H. (2012). Shame regulation in personality pathology. *Journal of Abnormal Psychology, 121*(2), 433.

Scheff, T. J. (1997). *Emotions, the social bond, and human reality: Part/whole analysis*. Cambridge: Cambridge University Press.

Tracy, J. L., Robins, R. W., & Tangney, J. P. (Eds.). (2007). *The self-conscious emotions: Theory and research*. New York: Guilford Press.

Wile, D. B. (2002). Collaborative couple therapy. In A. S. Gurman & N. S. Jacobson (Eds.), *Clinical handbook of couple therapy* (3rd ed., pp. 281–307). New York: Guilford Press.

# Chapter 3
# Communicating with Shame: Monitoring the Presence of Shame in Conversations

The relationship between shame and communication is interesting and in many ways tragic. When a person tries to communicate his shame, he will often do so in ways which either alienate or shame the other person. Whereas the most effective way to reduce shame is by means of talking, it is often through these same efforts that we hurt the other, leading to continual cycles of reciprocal shaming.

## 3.1 The Dangers of Conversing

Conversations can trigger shame almost instantaneously. This is especially evident when conversing about sensitive subjects, in which shame must be addressed and managed on a moment-by-moment basis. However, even discussing subject matter which is relatively emotion-neutral can activate a shame response.

Conversations are dangerous for a number of reasons. First, conversations are means for solving problems. Having a problem implies that someone failed and was unsuccessful or not competent enough. Because shame is a natural consequence of experiencing failure, every problem solving oriented conversation risks evoking shame in at least one of the participants. While the participants think they are focusing on the real problem and searching for appropriate solutions, the dominant issue has become the unregulated shame that was triggered by the conversation, dramatically affecting the outcome of it.

Second, conversations bring out a myriad of other emotions. Conversations can make us angry or sad or anxious. Since shame tends to bind to other emotions (Kaufman 1985), experiencing feelings that are not directly related to shame can, nonetheless, easily elicit a shame response.

Third, every conversation includes one party who will be talking more, explaining more, understanding more, wanting more, and so forth. This element of one person being/doing/wanting more than the other creates a power imbalance which



U. Weinblatt, *Shame Regulation Therapy for Families*,
https://doi.org/10.1007/978-3-319-77470-1_3

leads to a shame reaction. Because shame is related to the perception of power and to the constant evaluation of who is more powerful, as power shifts during the conversation, the person who feels himself to be in an inferior position will experience shame and retaliate.

So, despite the fact that people don't know exactly how shame influences their conversations, they do know the bottom line – conversations are risky and can make things worse. As a result, many will decide to avoid conversations altogether and try to deal with their problems on their own. However when people try to protect their relationship by remaining silent, they lose their voice and insert distance into their relationship, which can be no less shaming and destructive. Without conversations, we are deprived of the basic tool for shame management – being able to expose ourselves, be seen by others, and be given validation and support for who we are. Without conversations, we also lose the opportunity to become closer and more intimate and to experience belonging – the experiences that lead most to shame reduction.

## 3.2 The Benefits of Ineffective Communication

Conversations can hurt, but hurtful conversations have an important function – they are often the only way for people to reveal their shame. Painful conversations are a result of using negative communication behaviors such as blaming, name calling, and interrupting, to name a few. Yet, ironically, these unsuccessful communication strategies are often the only way for people to expose their shame (Wile 1993, 2008). Understanding these behaviors through this lens develops a capacity to effectively monitor the level of shame in the conversation and to empathize with instead of criticize or blame those using them (see Table 3.1).

## 3.3 The Irresistibility of Saying "You" Instead of "I"

Mother to son: *"You never clean your room!"*
Husband to wife: *"You don't care about me!"*
Teacher to student: *"You interrupt the class all the time!"*

We all know that good communication means focusing more on ourselves rather than on the other person. The mother, for example, would be communicating more effectively if she would say "I get frustrated when the room is not cleaned," and the husband would probably do better if he could say "I get sad when I think you don't care about me," and the teacher would also be in a better position had she said "I am angry at you because you interrupted the class today." Such statements would have been putting the spotlight on the emotion of the communicator instead of on the faulty behavior of the other. This would provide a better opportunity for the other to listen instead of just feeling accused.

**Table 3.1** The advantages and disadvantages of ineffective communication for regulating shame

| Communication practice | Possible advantages for regulating shame | Disadvantages for regulating shame |
|---|---|---|
| Saying "you" | A clue for the person that he is experiencing shame<br>An effort to converse | Shaming the other by criticizing him and as a result reducing his motivation to converse |
| Saying "never" and "always" | An authentic reflection of the intensity of experienced shame<br>A way to empower oneself<br>A way to capture attention | Shaming the other person by expressing a statement which is an inaccurate description and overexaggeration of things |
| Interruptions | Stopping a shaming communication | Shaming the other by stopping him as he is talking and not listening |
| Mind reading | An effort of knowing the other<br>A way to empower oneself | Shaming the other by assuming to know better than he does |
| Changing the subject/ bringing evidence from the past | A way of trying to experience influence<br>Trying to communicate more accurately | Shaming the other by reminding him of shaming events he would not be talked about |

What most people don't realize is that there is a more urgent motive for trying to limit the usage of saying "you." Since shame is the emotion most connected with identity and the protection of the self, when a person uses "you," they are entering into the domain of identity appraisal which immediately triggers a shame reaction in the other person. Of course not every usage of "you" creates shame. For example, "you are wonderful" or "you are sweet" will most likely elicit an opposite reaction of pride and a sense of recognition. Yet, they still involve the practice of defining the self. Therefore, it comes as no surprise that people with high levels of shame have a hard time tolerating even such positive statements. In an effort to not experience shame, they resist even affirmative words, leaving the people who conveyed these messages baffled and frustrated.

For these reasons, people engaged in conflict are often instructed by professionals to focus on themselves and to use the "I messages" instead of "you messages." Yet, even after diligent coaching, we cannot resist the temptation, and we continue, stubbornly, to use "you messages."

Asking people who are shamed not to use "you" is like asking an angry person not to raise their voice or a depressed person not to be sad. When we have shame, we think in sentences with "you" and feel the need to express this. The stronger the shame, the more urgent it is to communicate the "you."

If we look more closely at the three statements in the previous example, we can see that they are efforts, even if unsuccessful, to communicate to the other, "I am experiencing shame and suffering from it!" All three (mother, husband, and teacher) *are really interested in having a conversation*, but they don't know that they are experiencing shame, and even if they did know, they would not know how to express it.

The mother, husband, and teacher are unaware of their feelings of shame, although if asked, they would report that they feel hurt. What they think they are doing is communicating this hurt by stating facts. They are not aware of the accusation involved, and even if they were to become aware of it, they would not care. The biggest challenge of shame regulation is knowing that we are experiencing shame and not becoming ashamed by this knowledge. Using the word "you" is a crucial part in this process. Hearing ourselves using "you" provides vital information – it mirrors to us that we are experiencing shame. This knowledge gives us the opportunity to communicate differently.

## 3.4 Why "Never" and "Always" Are Not Always Bad

I remember that as a beginning therapist, I was very impressed with a lecture given by a communication skills expert and his work with couples and parents. He showed how using the words "never" and "always" leads to greater escalation and expressed the importance of stopping couples from using these words. That same week, I met with a couple who used to fight throughout most of our sessions. I introduced them to my newly acquired knowledge about the harm of using the words "always" and "never." They seemed to listen and agreed that such words are not helpful. Yet the moment they started arguing, "never" and "always" showed up. It did not matter how often I pointed out that they are violating the rules of good communication; they continued to do so. When I tried to prevent them from using these words, they became angry with me for not allowing them to express how they *were really* feeling. They said that I was pushing them to be dishonest and inauthentic.

Just as "you" statements are signs of the presence of shame, so are "never" and "always." When we forbid their presence in conversations, we can unknowingly diminish the participants' ability to expose their shame. Moreover, just as "you" is irresistible, so are "never" and "always." What makes "never" and "always" so tempting are three important features:

(a) They are a true reflection of the intensity of the shame feeling. While "never" and "always" are exaggerations (there will always be situations in which these superlatives will not be accurate), *they are true to the intensity of the feeling.* Using "never" and "always" is, therefore, a simple and economic way of expressing how frustrating and hurtful the other person's behavior really is.
(b) They are provocative and as such capture the other person's attention. This is essential because, for shame to be regulated, we need the other to be present with their full attention and understanding. A provocative statement that captures the other's attention provides an opportunity for such regulation.
(c) They empower the shamed person who is feeling powerless.

"Never" and "always" are powerful statements. When do we use such commanding statements? When we feel belittled, humiliated, and hurt or simply when we feel shame. Using these two words is a shortcut for empowerment. Combine these words with a "you," and now you have an authoritative combination:

"You always complain!"
"You are never satisfied!"

However, using such statements does not make us feel powerful for more than a few seconds. The victory over shame is short-lived for a number of reasons. First, such statements can easily be refuted:

Husband: "You always complain!"
Wife: "I didn't complain yesterday."

And second, such statements are provocative. They often shame the other person which leads them to counterattack with their own brand of shaming statements:

Wife: "You never do anything around the house!"
Husband: "And you are always unsatisfied!"

People with low levels of shame can express themselves without the need to use "never" and "always." They can do so, because they are not experiencing the inhibiting effects of shame. In Chap. 2, we have discussed how shame leads to "loss of voice" – to the inability to know and express one's experience fully. Without shame, the wife that complained "you never do anything around the house" could have said:

"You wouldn't believe how awful I felt when you didn't help me clean up the house. I felt as if you don't care about me. I felt alone, unloved. As time passed, I became really angry at you and thought that I will always be left with cleaning the house on my own."

However, those who are experiencing intense shame are in a different situation. For them, expressing themselves in such a way is not an option, even in a therapeutic setting. For them, using "never" and "always" is often the only way to free themselves, even for a few moments, from the painful effects of shame.

## 3.5 Interrupting Shame

I am sitting in a session with a mother and her 14-year-old daughter:

Mother: "You never talk to me about…"
Daughter (interrupting): "Because you are boring!"
Mother: "I am trying to say that…"
Daughter (interrupting): "You don't need to say it."
Mother: "But I really want to…"
Daughter (interrupting): "And I really don't!"

And now I am sitting with a couple:

He: "Today I want to talk about last weekend…"
She (interrupting): "You mean the one you did everything to..."
He (interrupting): "I did everything??? And what do you have to say about…"
She (interrupting): "Yes, you have a real talent for…"
He (interrupting): "Don't interrupt me. I want you to…"
She (interrupting): "I am not interrupting. I just want our therapist to know the truth."

We know that interruptions are not helpful. Interruptions impede communication by silencing the person who is talking, getting them angry, and goading them to take a negative position against whatever the interrupter is saying. Nonetheless, interrupting has some benefits, the most important being:

(a) The ability to stop a shaming process
(b) To let the other person know that the interrupter has reached their limits in listening

People interrupt because they are experiencing shame, and they feel that if they don't interrupt, they will experience even more shame. If they weren't experiencing shame, they might say:

"What you are saying is hurting me. Please stop talking like this; it will make things worse for us."

But since shame does not allow us to be so sophisticated, we are left with the ungraceful act of interrupting.

Interrupting also communicates that we have reached a point where we cannot listen any longer. In this sense it important information. If we refrain from interrupting the other person, we can easily disconnect from the conversation. So while we spared the other from experiencing the pain and frustration of being interrupted, we also left him on his own, talking all alone to himself.

Interrupting is a way to stop feeling shame. As with other shame-reducing strategies, the price is often high – it ignites the shame of the person who was interrupted. This leaves the person who is experiencing shame a choice between two options: refrain from interrupting the other and risk experiencing more shame (or just stop listening) or interrupt and increase the danger that the other person will retaliate because they are now the one experiencing shame. When people learn that their impulse to interrupt is a clue to the presence of their own shame, they can interrupt in a more constructive way. Thus instead of brushing off/silencing the other, they can say:

"What you are saying hurts me, but I don't want to interrupt you so I will wait until you finish."

This type of interruption is a compromise – it is still an interruption and, in that sense, helps the interrupting person to reduce some of their shame, yet it does not shame the person being interrupted in the same way.

## 3.6 Shame Is Not the Best Mind Reader

Shame is connected to how we think we are perceived in another person's mind (Gilbert 2003). The more shame we experience, the more we become obsessed with the intentions of the other and with their evaluation of us. Products of shame-induced mind reading include accusations such as:

"You think I am stupid"
"You never loved me"
"You want to leave me!"
"You hate me!"

When we feel shame, we need to know. We need to know why the other person hurts us and why we are suffering. This knowing has to be fulfilled because, without it, we feel less safe and more vulnerable. So, we start analyzing the other's intentions. Soon we feel that we know that other person's motivations better than they themselves do.

Let's take, for example, the situation in which a parent asked his son to do his homework and later discovered that his son did nothing about it. The following is the father's internal dialogue, reflecting his efforts to make sense of his son's behavior:

"Why is Tommy not doing his homework after I told him to do it *ten times*?"
"He doesn't care about what I say."
"He doesn't care about me! If he did, he would do his homework."
"And after everything that I did for him!"
"He thinks my sole job as a father is to provide his fun. He isn't willing to do anything difficult."
"But he was willing to make an effort when his friends asked him to!"
"Yes, it is just me that he doesn't take into account! I mean nothing to him!"

Clients are frequently instructed by therapists to ask the other directly instead of engaging in such mind reading. But when people are engaged in conflict, they cannot help themselves from thinking, guessing, and appraising what is happening in another person's mind. The problem with mind reading is not mind reading per se, but rather reading the other's mind incorrectly and proclaiming one's conclusion in a provocative manner.

As with the other ineffective shame regulation communication tactics, mind reading makes us feel strong. We are all familiar with movies portraying a very charismatic and wise psychologist, one who really knows what goes on in another person's mind. When we feel unsure, we like playing such powerful characters. And, as with other shame-reducing actions, this show of power is usually not accepted and appreciated by the other. No one likes another person to be the highest authority on who they are. Such confident statements provoke and shame the other person, who then feels like rebelling against such accusations.

A more constructive approach to mind reading treats these evaluations (or accusations) as, what Dan Wile calls, "rough drafts," which are a starting point for understanding one's experience. When a person says, "You think I am stupid!," we should view this as a first step, a first sketch of how this person is really feeling. We should appreciate that it is an effort on the communicator's side to expose their feelings. Helping that person to develop those statements leads to true reduction of shame. For example, helping the person to say "*I am afraid* that you think I am stupid" will be the next step in turning the initial "ineffective" mind reading act into a statement that has real power to regulate the person's shame.

## 3.7 The Need to Have Influence

When people are engaged in a heated discussion and start feeling inferior, they tend to engage in two additional empowering behaviors:

- They tend to bring up negative experiences from the past.
- They tend to change the subject and talk about something else.

Let's look at an example of the first type of behavior – bringing up negative experiences from the past:

Wife: "I really want us to go to Mexico for our family vacation."
Husband: "I told you I don't want to."
Wife: "It is always so hard with you! Why are you making it so difficult?"
Husband: "I am not making it difficult."
Wife: "It is just like 2 years ago when I organized our vacation to Greece. You made faces and gave everybody bad vibes."

The wife is trying to convince her husband to go to Mexico. Very quickly she feels that she is having no impact on him. Feeling powerless, she looks for more convincing arguments to try and make her point. Bringing up the vacation in Greece seems like a great move. What she is hoping for is that her husband will say:

Husband: "Yes, now that you mention it, I remember that I did behave like a jerk 2 years ago. You know what? This time I'll try to enjoy myself and do it differently. Let's go to Mexico and enjoy ourselves!"

Had he had said that, the wife's shame would quickly disappear for a number of reasons:

(a) He would be validating his wife's experience from 2 years ago.
(b) He would be apologizing for it.
(c) He would be admitting that he is difficult when it comes to family vacations.
(d) He would give her the feeling that she can influence him.

But instead, what he says is:

"You forced me to go on that trip to Greece too, but I don't remember making any faces."

which leads to the following response from the wife:

"And that picture from the Acropolis, you didn't make a face there???"

The wife started by trying to convince her husband to go with her on a vacation to Mexico, and now suddenly she finds herself trying to convince him that he really did make a face during the trip to Greece. Her original goal was not to talk about Greece but to show more powerful evidence, in order to feel that she can influence her husband. Bringing up the photo from the Acropolis is also a desperate effort to try to communicate her underlying feelings, namely, that it was humiliating for her to travel with someone who she thinks doesn't want to travel with her. Although seemingly irrelevant, the photo that surfaced as a result of the escalation process is actually of tremendous value. It crystallizes the experience of shame the wife is feeling.

In fights, bringing up the past is a tactic hardly ever exercised by only one side. Everyone has a long list of grievances and injustices to be used only in times of need. Waving the list feels empowering for a few moments, but as a strategy, bringing up the past continues to have the same effect that other anti-shame strategies have – they make the partner less willing to listen.

In trying to have more influence on the other, another related approach is to twist the argument to center around something altogether irrelevant:

Husband: "I don't remember you taking any pictures at the Acropolis."
Wife: "Are you serious? I am talking about the photo which is just next to the photos we took in that restaurant where we had that awful moussaka!"[1]
Husband: "Yes, that I remember very well. I hope you aren't blaming me for that restaurant! I told you we shouldn't eat there!"

What the husband and wife are doing is shifting to the second empowering devise – changing the subject. It started with the conversation switching from talking about the Mexico trip to talking about the picture taken on the Acropolis, and now the conversation has reached a new destination – the moussaka of their chosen restaurant.

Viewing the conversation from the outside can lead one to reach the conclusion that this new information is not helping the couple to move in the direction of resolving the argument. Actually, many couples therapists would stop the conversation at this point:

Therapist: "I think you are getting off track; lets return to your original conversation about the trip to Mexico."

[1] Moussaka is an eggplant-based dish, often including ground meat and béchamel sauce and is one of my wife's favorites.

While such a suggestion might reduce the escalation, reorient the couple, and cool things down for a few moments, it will also miss the most important aspect of what this couple is trying to do – to give voice to their experience of shame. In this sense, returning to the original conversation on Mexico will not move the couple forward and will probably lead the unregulated shame to show up in another disguise. So instead of stopping the conversation, I prefer to help each partner to make their point, in order to give voice to their shame. For example, I would help the husband to convey this message to his wife:

Husband: "What I am really trying to tell you is that I know that I become obnoxious when I feel forced to follow you. That is exactly what happened in that restaurant. I wish we could do more of what I want. Maybe then I would be a better travel companion to you and wouldn't whine whenever you take me to different places. It doesn't make me feel good to be like that."

And I would like to help the wife send this message:

Wife: "You know, I get really frustrated when I remember that restaurant. I insisted on eating there because I thought that it would really help you to enjoy yourself. The travel guide said that they have the best moussaka in Greece, and I know how much you like eating it. When you didn't enjoy that restaurant, I really felt like I can't do anything right."

What I am trying to do is to give voice to each partner's experience of powerlessness, helplessness, and isolation. In many ways I am trying to do the same thing that the partners are trying, ineffectively, to do, through the devices described in this chapter – using the words "you," "never," and "always," interrupting, mind reading, and bringing old grievances up from the past – that is, to express how they feel.

## 3.8 Knowing that Leads to Better Communication

Lewis referred to shame as a "sub-atomic particle that can be seen only by the traces it leaves behind" (Lewis 1992 pp. 34). Indeed because of the nature of shame – to create a smoke screen and conceal and hide its existence – we need clues that will allow us to detect its presence. Therefore, in this approach, clients are not requested to try and suppress their need to use communication strategies that lead to escalation but rather:

- To view these communication behaviors as signs that clients are experiencing shame
- To understand that they are a combination of effective and ineffective shame regulation behaviors
- To appreciate that they are effective in the sense that they reduce the level of shame for one person

- To know that these strategies are ineffective in that they will most likely offend the other person and make him or her feel shame
- To realize that these communication behaviors are "rough drafts" which need to be revised in order for them to maximize their emotional regulation and communication potential

Developing such a "third ear" that picks up on the clues that shame leaves behind is vital for the process of monitoring the level of shame in the system, on a moment-by-moment basis. Having a competent third ear allows therapists to address the presence of shame quickly, before it paralyzes the people having the discussion, and the therapists themselves.

## References

Gilbert, P. (2003). Evolution, social roles, and the differences in shame and guilt. *Social Research, 70*(4), 1205–1230.

Kaufman, G. (1985). *Shame: The power of caring*. Rochester, VT: Schenkman Books.

Lewis, M. (1992). *Shame, the exposed self.* New York: The Free Press.

Wile, D. B. (2008). *After the honeymoon: How conflict can improve your relationship*, (Revised ed). Oakland, CA: Collaborative Couple Therapy Books.

Wile, D. B. (1993). *After the fight: Using your disagreements to build a stronger relationship.* New York: Guilford Press.

# Chapter 4
# Systemic Mirroring: A Model for Shame Regulation

Sometimes we can feel awfully alone and at the same time feel as if the whole world is observing us and judging us. Indeed, when experiencing shame, no man is an island[1]:

Daughter: "I am going out."
Father: "It's already 20:00. Tomorrow is a school day; stay home."
Daughter: "No, I already made plans."
Father: "Sorry, but you can't."
Daughter: "My friends are waiting for me. You don't understand; they always make fun of me for not being able to go out! Why do I always have to be different? You never let me do anything. I hate you! I hate this family!"
Father (raising his voice): "You went out 2 days ago and this is your way of saying thank you?! I want you in your room! Now!"
Daughter (yelling and screaming, running to her room): "You never trust me. You don't love me and never did!"
Father: "Lower your voice! The whole neighborhood does not need to hear you!"
Daughter: "I don't care!"

Shame is the emotion where psychological and sociological processes meet. More than any other emotion, shame determines the quality of the bond we form with ourselves, as well as the bond we have with others who make up our social environment. It is this interaction between the relationships with one's self and with others (and others as a group) that makes shame dynamics so special. In the above example, the daughter felt humiliated and belittled by her father's refusal to let her go out. This reaction is intensified as a result of her belief that her friends will ridicule her for staying at home. She responds by shaming her father whose

[1] John Donne's saying, "no man is an island," highlights the importance of others to one's life and the interdependence between people. It is considered one of the most popular expressions in the field of family therapy, emphasizing that "we exist as parts of an interactional system" (Piercy et al. 1996).



U. Weinblatt, *Shame Regulation Therapy for Families*,
https://doi.org/10.1007/978-3-319-77470-1_4

shame is also escalating as a result of the embarrassment connected with the thought that the neighbors are hearing the fight and developing a negative attitude toward the family.

## 4.1 The Triple Effect of Shame

Drawing on Dan Wile's (2011) conceptualization, when we experience a strong shame reaction, three related problems arise:

- The individual's problem is loss of voice: we lose the ability to express what is most alive for us. It is a reduction in one's experience and reflects a disruption in the ability of the self to collaborate with and to integrate its constituent parts.
- The relational problem is loss of connection: we shift from a collaborative mode to an adversarial or disconnected mode. We lose the ability and the will to communicate with another, to recruit their support, and to cooperate and collaborate with them. Often, this means either wanting to hurt them or to disconnect from them.
- The observer's/group's problem is loss of empathy: in witnessing the shamed person's behaviors and relationships, others (i.e., any observing third person) become reproachful, disapproving, or alienating. In short, others lose the capacity to have empathy for him.

In the therapeutic setting, this triple effect plays out by the client losing his ability to adequately express his experience (loss of voice), the client losing his rapport with those family members present or with the therapist (loss of connection), and the therapist losing her own empathy toward the client (loss of empathy). The therapeutic task is to recover from these three losses. To do so, the therapist assists the individual in finding his or her voice, helps re-establish connections to significant others, and regains her own lost empathy for the client (and helps other observers to become empathetic to the main client).

### *4.1.1 The Problem of Shame on the Individual Level: Loss of Voice*

When people experience shame, they lose their capacity to articulate their feelings to others or even to themselves (Greenberg and Iwakabe 2011; Nathanson 1992). In Chap. 2, I described the three experiences that comprise this process:

(a) We do not know how we feel.
(b) If we do know how we feel, we do not want to admit it to others.
(c) Even if we are willing to admit our feelings, we do not know how to communicate them.

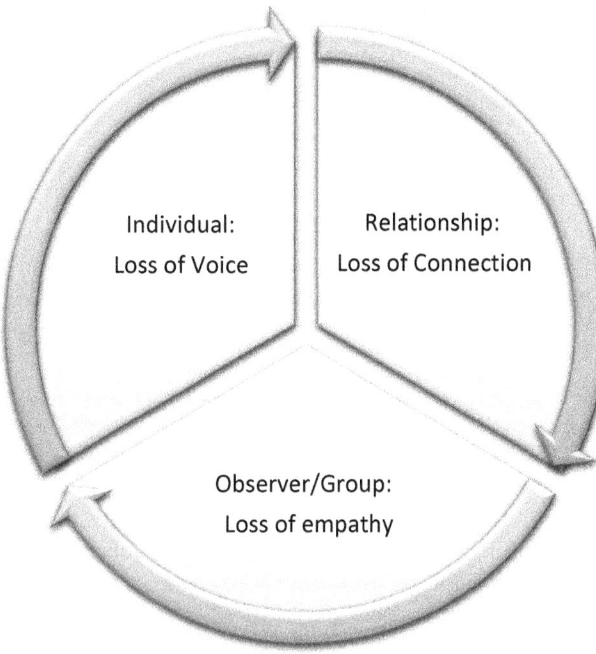


**Fig. 4.1** The triple effects of shame in the system

Losing voice does not necessarily mean that when we feel shame we become silent (although this may occur as well). Rather, it is often the other way around; we yell, scream, give lectures, explode, criticize, and – above all – blame. These behaviors reveal the constriction of our awareness and reveal our detachment from our underlying emotions. By losing voice, we lose the ability to express that which is most influential and important in the moment (Wile 1993). This means that at various times we lose one, or any combination, of the following: our ability to express our needs, our ability to express wishes, and our ability to express various emotions (Kaufman 1985). Whether this loss of voice is cloaked in provocative statements or shrouded in disconnection and silence, either strategy for regulating shame will lead to losses in connection and the loss of others' empathy (Figure 4.1).

### 4.1.2 *The Problem of Shame at the Relational Level: Loss of Connection*

The higher the person's shame level, the quicker his relationships shift from a collaborative mode to a hostile or disconnected mode of interaction.

Connection occurs when people can share, confide, and reveal their true feelings and the other person understands (Wile 2011). This is the true antidote for shame, for when we experience collaboration and love, we are immunized against feeling shame. Unfortunately, when we experience a strong shame reaction, we lose our ability to attain this connection, and instead we are driven to do the opposite: to hide and try to disconnect from the other and from ourselves or to attack the person who made us feel shame.

Attacking behaviors[2] have the function of transferring shame from one person to the other and contain the same wish, "I want you to feel how I feel." When we criticize, disapprove, belittle, degrade, devalue, or take revenge on, we are investing great effort in trying to get the other to "understand" something, namely, that we have been shamed and are not going to allow it to happen again. We often feel that the message been received only after the other shows signs of being shamed (Keltner et al. 1997).

Disconnection can be manifested in subtle ways, like talking about insignificant matters, or becoming immersed in daily distractions, like working on the computer or watching TV. Disconnection can also be observed through more obvious signs: trying to numb oneself through drinking beer, becoming silent, physically distancing from the other, or becoming immersed in a fantasy world like porn sites and computer games. All of these behaviors are independent efforts (compared to the "dependent" effort of attacking) that try to minimize or completely render shame.

### *4.1.3 The Problem of the Observer/Group: Loss of Empathy*

Shame is a public phenomenon that elicits evaluations from inner and outer critics. Indeed, it is difficult to remain nonjudgmental when a person switches to the attack and/or disconnect modalities. Behaviors of contempt, bullying, devaluing, and ignoring naturally elicit reactions from the social milieu that communicate the message "This needs to stop" (Weinblatt 2013). However, the more intense the shame reactions (disconnecting or attacking), the more dysfunctional these voices become; instead of leading to a reduction in problematic behaviors, they lead to an increase in such behaviors and to an escalation of the shame due to social rejection and stigma.

Moreover, the stronger the shame, the more evaluations flood one from within. The person experiencing shame lives in both a private and a public world full of criticism. There is nothing that he or she can do which does not elicit disparaging inner commentary such as "Look at you; you are disgusting," "You are not good enough," or "You should not exist" (Potter-Efron 2011). The therapeutic task is to help shift the observers (inner and outer) from a position of criticalness and alienation to one of empathy. In the therapy room that means the therapist herself needs to find a way to recover from losing her empathy to the client.

---

[2] Of course not all attacking behaviors are shame related. Attacks can be fueled by other emotions such as fear or anger, and their function in these cases is different.

## 4.2 The Systemic Mirroring Intervention

Mirroring and reflection is one of the fundamental tools used by therapists and educators from all therapeutic orientations for regulating feelings and enhancing relationships. It is the main medium for communicating the message "I see you" and "you are not alone." It is through mirroring that relationships become attuned and synchronized. It is also through this course that individual identity develops and becomes integrated (Schore 1994).

As a metaphor for understanding psychological processes, the mirror has a long history of usage (Kohut 1971). The metaphor is still being used extensively in understanding the most basic process of emotional regulation and attachment (Fonagy and Target 1997). In the past 20 years, the mirror symbology in traditional psychology has been reinforced and validated by an exciting discovery in neuroscience – the discovery of mirror neurons. Mirror neurons are neurons that mirror the activities of someone we are watching by activating similar regions in our own brains. Thus, when one person observes another performing an action or experiencing a feeling, they are, on a neurological level, feeling as if they were doing the same activity. It is through the activation of these neurons that we become empathetic to others – that we feel what they feel (Gallese 2001). It is with these neurons that we develop the ability to understand others and to understand ourselves. Not surprisingly, it has been hypothesized that mirror neurons also play a major role in the development and regulation of self-conscious emotions such as pride, guilt, and shame.

### *4.2.1 A Pain-Regulating Intervention*

Since shame is experienced as intense pain, in order to treat shame, we need to have a method that will regulate the pain involved. Without it, people drop out of therapy because the pain that is generated during therapy is too much for them to bear. The systemic mirroring intervention is inspired by a physical pain management method called "mirror therapy." Mirror therapy is a physiotherapeutic procedure for treating "phantom limb" – the chronic and intensely painful sensation experienced by many amputees.

The primary device of this therapy is a mirror box,[3] from which the patient gets visual feedback that trains the brain to reorganize information about the injured part of the body (Ramachandran and Rogers-Ramachandran 1996; Ramachandran and Altschuler 2009). The mirror box device is composed of a box with a divider bisecting it and a mirror attached to the divider, facing one chamber. The typical procedure involves placing the good limb into the side with the mirror and the injured

[3] Invented by Ramachandran, a neuroscientist and one of the biggest proponents of mirror neurons

limb into the other chamber. The person then looks into the mirror on the side with the good limb and makes various movements with it. Because the person is seeing the reflected image of the good hand moving, it appears as if the phantom limb is also moving. Phantom limbs are often perceived by the amputee to be clenched or bent at uncomfortable angles (as they may have been just prior to amputation). Through the use of this visual feedback, it becomes possible for the patient to "move" the phantom limb and to thereby "set it" into a position which would be less painful, were it still there.

In the systemic mirroring intervention, we try to do something similar: by speaking as if we are the client and having him watch us while we assume his identity, we hope that the person receiving an improved mirror image of himself will regain some of the psychological capabilities which had been inhibited by his shame.

### 4.2.2 From Dyad to Triad

When we speak of classical mirroring, we usually think of two people: the parent and child, husband and wife, and therapist and client. The systemic mirroring approach expands the traditional dyadic mirroring interaction to a triadic mirroring one. In this approach, mirroring is (optimally) done with three people in the counseling room: a counselor (therapist, school counselor) and two clients (parent and child, couple, two siblings, teacher and student, etc.). This leads to a process of mirroring which is more complex and which produces more effective emotional regulation, especially when dealing with shame.

The rationale for viewing the triad as the basic unit for shame regulation in therapy is based on the idea of the triple effect of shame. Since shame is experienced on three levels (the self, the relationship, and the observer), having three people in the room allows this dynamic to be fully actualized.

### 4.2.3 Speaking for the Person as a Way to Resolve the Triple Effects of Shame

The technique of speaking for one of the clients has a rich tradition in psychotherapeutic work. Originally Moreno called it "doubling" in psychodrama, garnering the attention of many relational-oriented therapists, who then referred to it as "becoming" (Snyder 1995), or "doubling-doubling" (Atkinson 2005), to name a few. Recently, it has been used in various parent-child dyadic treatments (Becker-Weidman and Hughes 2008). In my own view, the most creative use of the technique was developed by Wile (1993, 2011). The technique is simple and starts by asking permission from one of the clients "to jump into his (or her) shoes":

> *"You said something important. May I try to say it as if I were you, in order to check whether I understood you correctly? If I get it wrong, please correct me."*

After receiving permission, the therapist looks at the other client and voices what he heard:

*"Ok, what I thought I heard your partner (or father, mother, son, teacher etc.) say is, 'I ...'."*

After finishing the sentence, the therapist looks back at the client he was speaking for and checks the validity of the therapist's statement:

*"So, did that sound like what you wanted to communicate?"*

If the client says "no," or "not quite," then he is asked to revise what the therapist said to make it more accurate.

If he indicates that the therapist's rendition truly reflects his feelings, then the other person is asked to reply to the statement that the therapist made while role-playing.

I use this intervention whenever I detect the presence of shame in the room. The technique is of tremendous importance in regulating shame for two major reasons. The first is that by the therapist speaking for the clients, a process of shame regulation can occur on all three levels previously described:

- By speaking for the client, the therapist can counter the loss of voice by introducing feelings, wishes, and needs that have been censored by shame.
- By speaking for the client, the therapist can soften the message, thereby allowing the other person to be exposed to it without becoming defensive and losing connection.
- By speaking for the client, the therapist is "forcing" himself to develop empathy for the client, thus replenishing his own lost or diminished empathy.

The second reason for its powerful impact on shame regulation stems from the unique constellation of images and reflections that are produced with this technique. Let us look at an example in which a therapist meets with an adolescent and his mother. The therapist has just heard a provocative/shame-triggering message from the son to the mother. Before she can answer, the therapist jumps in, looks at the adolescent, and asks his permission to talk as if she were him. Then the therapist looks at the mother and begins talking (see Fig. 4.2):

Let us look more closely at what is happening for each one of the participants. The adolescent's first response is *curiosity*, thinking to himself "I wonder how the therapist is going to represent me?" This immediately regulates some of his shame because curiosity counteracts a shame response. The adolescent is looking at the therapist representing him but is not met with the eyes of the therapist. This makes it easier for the adolescent to regulate his shame.[4] Then the adolescent *compares* his own experience to that which was represented. When experiencing shame, cognitive comparison processes always ignite (Gilbert 2000). Often such comparisons result in the experience of failing to meet a standard and will cause a downward

[4] This recess from eye contact is a crucial aspect of the systemic mirroring approach. The discrepancy between the success rates of dyadic and triadic interventions can be attributed in part to the latter's allowing the client a moment of relative privacy while he learns about himself through watching this reflection of his hidden needs, without his reactions being overtly observed.

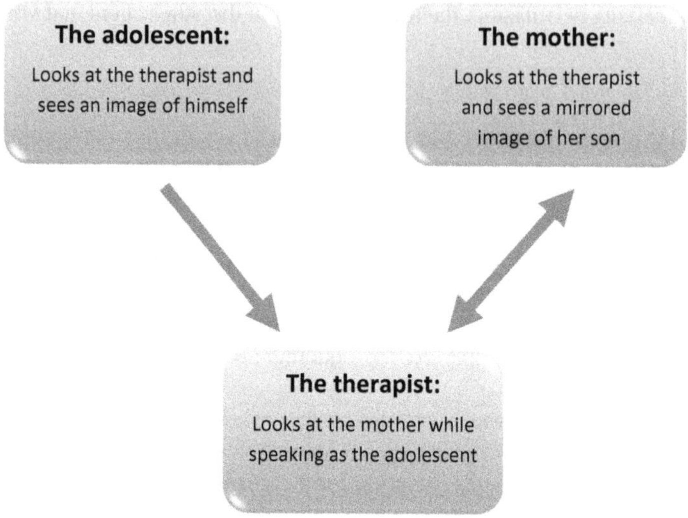


**Fig. 4.2** The reflections in systemic mirroring intervention

spiral of emotions. By having the adolescent compare himself to the slightly better image that has just been presented, we neutralize this process. On that note, when representing the client, one should aim to present him as only a little bit better and remain within his possible experiences. Therapists with good intentions, who too quickly try to represent the client in an overly positive way, leave the clients feeling misunderstood and alone.

The mother at this time does some comparing of her own. She compares the message she hears from the therapist with her own beliefs about her son. Because the therapist communicates with her as her child, and because she speaks in ways that move them closer, she becomes more connected to her son/therapist. Although it seems like the therapist is on the adolescent's side (she represents him), she maintains direct eye contact with the mother. In that way, all three are connected. By representing the adolescent, the therapist repairs also the critical position that was starting to develop toward him, thus preventing an increasingly critical stance within herself from snowballing into a loss of empathy for the teenager. By representing the adolescent, the therapist is, in many ways, disappearing from the session. This disappearance is helpful; there is no need for a critical and unempathetic therapist in the room.

### 4.2.4 *An Example of Regulating Shame in Parent-Child Conflict*

The systemic mirroring intervention requires having three people in the room. When the client is a child or an adolescent, and the parents ask who should join him for the first session, I either say "The parent he feels safest with" or "The parent who is most verbose." In the second session, I usually see the child with the other parent. Then, for the rest of the therapy, I do not switch between parents, but rather, invite the one parent who is most consistently available.[5]

Let us jump into a session I had with a mother and her 15-year-old son. We are only a few minutes into the session when the mother says:

Mother: "I told him to clean up his room, and he did nothing, nothing at all. He's always like that; he does only what *he* wants!"
Son: "Do this! Do that! You're always on my back, and I'm sick of it!"
Mother: "And I am sick of you turning the house into a filthy place!"

The conversation has only just begun, but it is quickly escalating. Neither side is representing their positions in terms that the other can hear, and both are using hurtful, degrading language (loss of voice). Experiencing shame in the moment and the memory of the event itself (which contributes its own shame) combine to create an accumulative shame response. They are attacking each other, and shame is transferred repeatedly between them. As observer/therapist, I am noticing that I am starting to lose my empathy toward both. I am thinking to myself, "Why is the cleanliness of his room more important to this mother than the way she relates toward her son?," and also, "This kid is so disrespectful; no wonder his mother is all over him." So, in order to prevent the mother and son from doing any more damage to each other, and in order for me to avoid being consumed by my critical thinking, I must intervene:

Therapist (looking at both): "OK I think you are both trying to say something important, and I want to see whether I understand you correctly. So I am going to jump into your shoes, and speak as if I am you, and then you let me know if I'm going in the right direction, or if I'm way off base."
Therapist (looking at mother): "I'll begin with you mom, and I'll try to voice what I heard you say. Since I have known you for only a short while, there is a good chance that I will make a mistake. If that's the case, please correct me at the end, ok?"
Therapist (looking at son): "So, what I think I heard your mother say to you was, 'I am so tired of having these fights with you. It's really exhausting'."
Therapist (looking at mother): "Is that what you meant?"
Mother (looking less angry and sadder): "Yes, it's awful."
Therapist (to son): "What's your response to that?"
Son: "I don't know why she has to come barging into my room like that. I didn't do anything to her. She always comes in with 'do this' and 'do that'."

I wish the son had not used "always" in that last sentence, as I know it will shame his mother. Yet, this "always" is also a clue, revealing the son's unregulated shame. By him saying "always," he has reminded me that I need to work harder to expand on what he is saying, to give his voice a richer quality.

Therapist (looking at mother): "Alright, and what I think your son was saying is 'I am tired of these fights too. But when you come in and surprise me like that, I don't like it'."

[5] In this regard, I knowingly choose not to adhere to classical family therapy theory.

Therapist (looking at son): "Is that what you meant?"
Son: "Yes, she wants me to immediately do whatever she says."

I think to myself, I really wish he hadn't said "immediately," and before I can finish my thought, I hear the mother shout:

Mother: "'Immediately?!' I asked you nicely at least five times before I came in! I said 'please', and even brought you a glass of Coke, but that didn't help anything! 'Immediately?!' Really?! I can't believe this; you are so...."

One of the good things about managing shame regulation is that it keeps you alert and ready. If I do not intervene now, the mother will say something that will evoke her son's shame, then later her own, and possibly even mine. So, I need to act quickly before the mother can end the sentence.

Therapist (looking at mother): "Ok, Ok, sorry for interrupting you, but I thought you just said something which I want to voice, alright?"

And without waiting for permission, I continue:

Therapist (looking at son): "What I heard your mother say is 'Listening to your last words, it sounds as if I am a terrible mother who just demands that you obey my orders all day. I think that's not a fair description of me'."
Therapist (looking at mother): "Does that make any sense?"
Mother: "Yah, sometimes it seems like he thinks I'm a witch."
Therapist (looking at son): "And your thoughts or feelings about that?"
Son (becomes quiet for 10 seconds): "I don't know."

These moments of hesitation are common in the process of regulating shame. They often occur when the person shifts from the adversarial/attacking mode to either a disconnected mode or a collaborative mode. In these moments, it is important to keep the process going.

Therapist (looking at son): "I thought that behind those words, there was more; may I voice it for you?"
Son: "Sure."
Therapist (looking at mother): "I'm guessing here, but if I had been your son, I would be feeling something like 'I did not deliberately refuse to clean the room; it's not as if I did it on purpose to get you angry'."
Son (quieter): "Yes, she thinks I am against her, but I'm not."
Therapist (looking at mother): "And your response to this is...?"
Mother (quiet for a few seconds): "I know that he's not against me... but why is it such a big deal to clean up his room?"

The mother and son are having a more connected and collaborative conversation. However, with the mother's last remark, they could easily slide back to a hostile interaction. So, again, I need to intervene:

Therapist (looking at son): "What I thought your mother really meant was 'I really don't like fighting with you either, it really isn't a pleasure for me. I know that

it's your room, and although I understand that it doesn't bother you when it's dirty, it would still be great if you would clean it up every now and then'."
Therapist (to son): "And your response to that?"
Son: "I do clean it up sometimes."

We have reached a crossroad. If the mother's shame is still under-regulated, she will respond with an attack – maybe a cynical remark like "You are absolutely right, cleaning once a month is technically 'sometimes'…." But, if the mother's shame is better regulated, she will, at that moment, be able to acknowledge the instances when he had been helpful. She will experience his last sentence as a request for appreciation. Luckily, this is exactly how she feels:

Mother: "He is right."

The mother just said the three magic words for shame regulation: "You are right." Seeing that her son is looking at her with a softer expression, she is encouraged to continue:

Mother (to therapist): "Yes, sometimes he does clean his room. The problem is that a few hours later, it reverts to its original state of chaos and looks as if he'd had a wild party in there (smiling)."

The smile, and the sense that the mother is suddenly enjoying the moment, is an indication that her shame is being regulated. The son who has just received acknowledgment from his mother has also now entered a collaborative state:

Son (smiling, looking at mother): "Yeah, she never lets me have parties in there. (looking at therapist) Can you tell her to let me have parties in my room (smiling)?"

## 4.3 Monitoring the Level of Shame in the Conversation

As the last example demonstrates, assessing the level of shame in the system on a moment-by-moment basis is crucial. Although I actually view the level of shame as a continuum, to simplify things, I will illustrate it here as a dichotomy: a regulated collaborative mode and an unregulated adversarial or disconnected mode (see Table 4.1).

In regulated shame states, people are curious and willing to learn and to admit their own part in fights. They make efforts to reconcile, often using humor. They have perspective and are able to evaluate their behavior and the behavior of people around them from a higher viewpoint. When people enter an unregulated shame state, they avoid, become silent, and withdraw, or they attack, accuse, blame, interrupt, and erroneously interpret the other's intentions. They lose their ability to enjoy, to be curious, and to learn from or get help from others.

Relationships shift constantly between regulated and unregulated shame states. We can be cruising along in a regulated shame state and, then a minute later, be

**Table 4.1** Markers of regulated and unregulated states

| | Regulated shame | Unregulated shame |
|---|---|---|
| Curiosity | V | |
| Excitement | V | |
| Admitting | V | |
| Blaming | | V |
| Willing to learn | V | |
| Silence | | V |
| Intimacy/connection | V | |
| Empathy | V | |
| Rage | | V |
| Interrupting | | V |
| Cynicism | | V |
| Resistance | | V |

triggered into a high shame state. Often these transitions occur unexpectedly; at times they may even flip counter to what everybody had anticipated. As an example, let us peer into a conversation I had with a couple whom I had been seeing because the husband had an affair. After 6 months of therapy, we had the following conversation:

Wife (to husband): "In order to move on, what I need from you is for you to take full responsibility for your actions; no more excuses and blaming our marriage."

During every session for the prior 6 months, the wife had, in various ways, requested this accountability. The husband, because of his own shame, hadn't been able to give her what she wanted; he had always hidden behind an assortment of excuses and rationales. But this day was different, and he finally accepted full liability:

Husband: "I shouldn't have done it, and I take full responsibility for it. Even if I was unhappy with our marriage, it was the wrong thing to do. I should have talked with you, communicated with you; we could have gone to therapy. Having an affair was a bad solution. I'm sorry."

I was moved. I was happy for the wife, happy for the husband who was finally able to say all of that, and happy about my abilities as a therapist. But suddenly, I looked at the wife and noticed that her response was different from what I would have expected it to be. Her face had lost its emotional expression, and she became silent. I could see that her reaction was negatively affecting the husband. Before I could react, I heard the husband say:

Husband: "You see?! Nothing satisfies her; she will always be angry with me. I think she likes being that way."

Just a moment earlier, I had been thinking that this therapy would have a wonderful Hollywood ending with me as the Oscar-winning director. I was proud of the wife, and of the husband, and of myself. Yet, only a minute had passed and I was starting to become critical, thinking to myself "Maybe he is right. Maybe she will never get over the affair. Maybe she can't let go of this anger." I was also thinking some critical thoughts about myself, "Who was I kidding when I embarked on therapy with these two? Maybe I should have sent them to my colleague who's an expert on relationship recovery after affairs. This is not what I am good at. It was wrong for me to take them on as my own clients."

What happened? The system shifted from a regulated shame state to an unregulated shame state. Hearing what the husband said had caused the wife to lose her voice, which led the couple to lose its connection, which led me to lose my empathy. I needed to do something quickly, or shame would have intensified. Luckily, I had an idea:

Therapist (to wife): "I can see that you have become silent. If I had been in your place, I might have reacted similarly, and I would have had a few thoughts in my mind. Is it ok if I say them?"

Wife: "Yes, you can say them."

Therapist (to husband): "If I were your wife, these are some of the things that might have been going through my mind: 'I appreciate what you have just said. Actually, I've wanted to hear this from you for a very long time. But for some reason, hearing it right now is not making me happy like I had expected it would. I know I should be happy, but I also have these other thoughts, like 'Why did it take you so long to take responsibility? Why couldn't you have done that immediately after I discovered the affair?' At the same time, don't get me wrong, I understand the importance of what you did today'."

Therapist (to wife): "Am I on the right track?"

Wife: "You're right. I wanted to hear that for so long. We had to go through half a year of therapy in order for him to say it. But you are also right about me acknowledging the importance of him saying it now. I just don't want him to think that I should be happy about it."

The wife regained her voice, which led to reconnection with the husband:

Therapist (to husband): "And what is your response to that?"

Husband: "I understand that I shouldn't expect her to be 'all smiles' about what I said. She has a right to be angry with me. I just hope that we can have a normal life again."

Sometimes, I like to add a question mark to someone else's shame evoking statement, as a way of turning it into a question that reduces shame. Thus, I say:

Therapist (to wife): "What I heard from your husband was a question, which is "Do you think that we will ever be able to live a normal life, without my betrayal hovering over our heads?"

Wife: "I hope so, and I am really trying."

Again, I wanted to turn the wife's statement into a question:

Therapist (to husband): "And now, what I just heard your wife ask is, 'Can you see that I am trying? Can you see my efforts?' "

Husband (to both): "Absolutely. And I want to tell you that it's making me appreciate you more every day. I am lucky to have you."

Now the husband had regained his voice, and I had regained my empathy. I was thinking to myself that this couple had come a long way in working through the affair, and once again, I was feeling hopeful that they could establish a good relationship between them. We had shifted back to a regulated shame state.

To summarize, the specialized tools in the systemic mirroring are:

- Working as a triad
- Being vigilant for the client's shame symptoms, such as using exaggerated superlatives or withdrawing
- The therapist assisting the client in voicing that which is silenced
- Managing eye contact in ways which balance under- and overexposure
- Reclaiming cognitive processes that shame hijacked
- Searching for words that shift relationship dynamics from disconnection and hostility to connection
- Monitoring the therapist's shame symptoms, and recuperating quickly, from states of loss of empathy

These tools allow therapists to effectively tackle the triple effects of shame. Yet, the process of shifting from unregulated to regulated shame states is not linear. Edna Fosha (2004) has said, "Nothing that feels bad is ever the last step," and in the course of regulating shame, feeling bad can turn to feeling good, which can then turn to feeling bad again. The process of shame regulation is often a roller-coaster ride which demands that people hold on while intermittently closing and opening their eyes.

## References


Atkinson, B. J. (2005). *Emotional intelligence in couples therapy. Advances from neurobiology and the science of intimate relationship*. New York: W. W. Norton & Company.

Becker-Weidman, A., & Hughes, D. (2008). Dyadic developmental psychotherapy: An evidence-based treatment for children with complex trauma and disorders of attachment. *Child & Family Social Work, 13*(3), 329–337.

Fosha, D. (2004). 'Nothing that feels bad is ever the last step': the role of positive emotions in experiential work with difficult emotional experiences. *Clinical Psychology & Psychotherapy, 11*(1), 30–43.

Fonagy, P., & Target, M. (1997). Attachment and reflective function: Their role in self-organization. *Development and Psychopathology, 9*(04), 679–700.

Gallese, V. (2001). The 'shared manifold' hypothesis. From mirror neurons to empathy. *Journal of Consciousness Studies, 8*(5–6), 33–50.

Gilbert, P. (2000). The relationship of shame, social anxiety and depression: The role of the evaluation of social rank. *Clinical Psychology & Psychotherapy, 7*(3), 174–189.

Greenberg, L. S., & Iwakabe, S. (2011). Emotion-focused therapy and shame. In R. L. Dearing & J. P. Tangney (Eds.), *Shame in the therapy hour* (pp. 69–89). Washington, DC: American Psychological Association.

Kaufman, G. (1985). *Shame: The power of caring*. Rochester, VT: Schenkman Books.

Keltner, D., Young, R. C., & Buswell, B. N. (1997). Appeasement in human emotion, social practice, and personality. *Aggressive Behavior, 23*(5), 359–374.

Kohut, H. (1971). *The analysis of the self: A systematic approach to the psychoanalytic treatment of narcissistic personality disorders*. New York: International Universities Press.

Nathanson, D. L. (1992). *Shame and pride: Affect, sex, and the birth of the self.* New York: WW Norton & Company.

Piercy, F. P., Sprenkle, D. H., & Wetchler, J. L. (1996). *Family therapy sourcebook.* New York: Guilford Press.

Potter-Efron, R. T. (2011). Therapy with shame-prone alcoholic and drug-dependent clients. In R. L. Dearing & J. P. Tangney (Eds.), *Shame in the therapy hour* (pp. 219–235). Washington, DC: American Psychological Association.

Ramachandran, V. S., & Rogers-Ramachandran, D. (1996). Synaesthesia in phantom limbs induced with mirrors. *Proceedings of the Royal Society of London B: Biological Sciences, 263*(1369), 377–386.

Ramachandran, V. S., & Altschuler, E. L. (2009). The use of visual feedback, in particular mirror visual feedback, in restoring brain function. *Brain, 132*(7), 1693–1710.

Schore, A. N. (1994). *Affect regulation and the origin of the self: The neurobiology of emotional development.* London: Psychology Press.

Snyder, M. (1995). "Becoming": A method for expanding systemic thinking and deepening empathic accuracy. *Family Process, 34*(2), 241–253.

Weinblatt, U. (2013). Die Regulierung des Schamgefühls bei intensiven Eltern-Kind-Konflikten: Praktiken des gewaltlosen Widerstands, die die Öffentlichkeit einbeziehen (Regulating shame in intense parent – child conflict through public opinion interventions in NVR therapy). *Familiendynamik: Systemische Praxis und Forschung, 38*(1), 62–71.

Wile, D. B. (1993). *After the fight: Using your disagreements to build a stronger relationship.* New York: Guilford Press.

Wile, D. B. (2011). Collaborative couple therapy: Turning fights into intimate conversations. *Psychotherapy in Australia, 17*(3), 52.

# Chapter 5
# Regulating the Shame of Parents: Helping Them to Become the Best Team They Can Be

We live in a culture that holds very high expectations of parents. They are supposed to be warm, supportive, encouraging, and tough, have excellent communication skills, possess basic knowledge of child development, and be able to set boundaries and know when to set them. They are also supposed to have deep, meaningful, enriching, and satisfying relationships with their children. With such high standards, it is no wonder that many parents feel inadequate and often feel shame in their parenting (Brown 2015).

While parents are extremely vulnerable to experiencing shame, they also have a built-in advantage in regulating shame, namely, the advantage of being two.[1] Parents' greatest resource for shame regulation is their relationship with each other. When parents work well as a team, give each other supportive feedback, and comfort each other after having a painful fight with the child, they provide the nurturance that keeps shame at bay. The capacity to turn the parental relationship into a source of advice, empowerment, and mutual soothing is dependent upon the parents' capability to regulate each other's shame. When parents find it difficult to do so and, instead, argue, criticize, and accuse each other, they turn what should have been an advantage into a disadvantage (Weinblatt 2013).

## 5.1 The Central Role of the Parents' Relationship in Regulating Shame in the Family

Parents have a distinct relationship with each other around their parenting (Weissman and Cohen 1985). This relationship is considered separate from the romantic and sexual aspects of the marriage and can be defined as the extent to which partners either

[1] I Focus in this chapter on two parent households. Single parents may come by the two-person advantage from elsewhere – a grandparent or friend or caregiver.



U. Weinblatt, *Shame Regulation Therapy for Families*,
https://doi.org/10.1007/978-3-319-77470-1_5

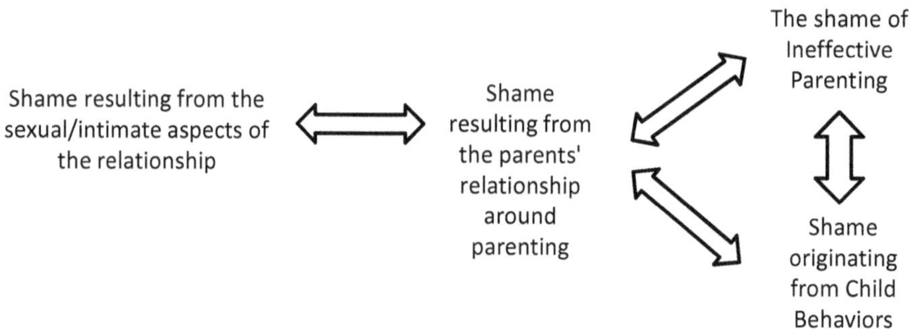


**Fig. 5.1** The centrality of the parents' relationship in family dynamics

support or undermine each other in dealing with their children (Feinberg 2003). The parenting alliance is highly sensitive and can easily be impacted, whether by the couple's relationship, the quality of parenting, or by the child's behavior (see Fig. 5.1). The experience of failure, in even one of these domains, is enough to immerse the parents' relationship in shame. For example, when parents experience a failure in their parenting (feeling ineffective, lacking influence, behaving in ways which contradict their own values) or when the child is failing (misbehaving, acting out, getting bad grades, socially unsuccessful, diagnosed with a medical, dental, developmental, or psychiatric problem), the parents can easily find themselves blaming each other for these failures.

Research on the parenting alliance has revealed the importance of this relationship in stabilizing aspects of family dynamics, including the quality of the partners' romantic life, the efficacy of parenting, and the child's behavior (McHale et al. 2004), and identified two major ingredients which contribute to a successful relationship between parents: communication/teamwork and respect (Konold and Abidin 2001). "Teamwork" refers to the amount of agreement reached concerning goals for disciplining the child. When teamwork is present, parents state "Talking to my partner about our child is something that I look forward to." "Respect" refers to trust in the other parent's commitment to and judgment regarding the care of the child. Respect is demonstrated in numerous ways, all of which imply appreciation for the other's good parenting and experienced by the other parent as having communicated the message "I believe that you, my partner, are a good parent." Not surprisingly, teamwork (the ability to collaborate) and respect are two key manifestations of regulated shame.

Respect is of key importance because, in parent-child relationships, shame is often distilled from the relational experience of being disrespected and unappreciated. In more extreme forms, the experience ferments into being unloved or even hated (Pattison 2000; Miller 1985). Indeed, it is often the need for more respect that brings parents to therapy in situations of intense conflict with their child. In these situations, it is quickly apparent that behind the wish for the child to obey the parent and to accept their authority lays the pain of feeling unappreciated, uncared for, and unloved by the child. This is often the child's experience too.

The centrality of the parents' relationship in the family places the parents in a position in which they can contain and, together, manage experiences of disrespect and shame that are produced in various domains of family life. Since this is no easy task, the parents' relationship itself tends to shift constantly from a regulated shame state in which the parents support, encourage, and respect the efforts of the other to an unregulated shame state in which the parents blame, criticize, and feel disrespected by each other. When this occurs, the centrality of the parents' relationship becomes a liability (Belsky et al. 1996); the parental relationship transforms from the original regulating haven it could have been to an exposed battleground, on which both sides painfully shame each other.

## 5.2 A Dilemma for Therapists

Parental fights are the clearest sign that the parents are not managing shame effectively, and it is through these same fights that parents are giving therapists opportunities to help them regulate their shame. Unfortunately, therapists (and I include here all helping professionals who are involved in parent training) don't like it when parents begin to fight during a session. They fear that the parental conflict might lead to a loss of focus, demoralization, and a disruption to the structure of the parent training process. This fear makes sense because, often, that is exactly what happens:

Therapist: "So tell me what brings you here today?"
Mother: "It is our son. He is so disrespectful. He curses us, does what he wants, and we think he is using drugs."
Father: "You think he is using drugs…"
Mother: "Right, I think so. You have the tendency to not see anything…"
Father: "And you have a tendency to always see everything. You are smothering him and constantly all over him. No wonder he behaves like that."
Mother: "Well if you would become just a little more involved, I wouldn't need to play the role of two parents!"
Father: "Nobody told you to act like two parents. Stop playing the Martyr!"
Mother: "I will, when you start behaving like a father!"

When such interactions occur, therapists can easily find themselves with a dilemma regarding how to move forward. The therapist's internal debate often includes thoughts such as:

- "Maybe what these parents need is to start couples therapy before starting parent training."
- "Maybe I'll send them to couples therapy, and at the same time, I'll do the parent training with them."
- "I need to find a way to cool them down and help them to refocus their attention on their parenting, and on their relationship with their child. I need to let them know that my office is not a place to have such fights."

And while each option has some advantages, they are all based on the notion that parent training (focusing on the child and on the parent-child relationship) and couple therapy (focusing on the relationship between the partners) are in many ways independent practices.

This assumption is also supported by the professional literature on family therapy. In the past 40 years, the field of family therapy has undergone a process of specialization that led to the emergence of two major domains of expertise: couple therapy and parent training. In this process, therapies designed specifically for resolving the main concerns of each subsystem were developed, resulting in impressive empirical outcomes for both couple therapy and parent training. At the same time, the split between the parenting system and the couple system has created new therapeutic challenges, one being the question of how to respond to marital fights while doing parent training.[2] These fights tend to fall in between the parent training domain and the couple therapy domain, leaving professionals questioning themselves as to whether this is a couple issue or a parenting issue.

Understanding parent to parent conflict as a clue to the presence of underregulated shame allows us to transcend the dichotomy of parenting vs. couples thinking. *According to this approach, it is the level of shame in the parents' relationship that determines whether we as therapists should focus on the parents' teamwork/communication or on the parenting skills.* When shame is unregulated, we should focus on the parents' relationship with each other and primarily on the parents' mutual shame regulation activities. As soon as shame is regulated, we can shift our attention to improving parenting skills/techniques. Ultimately, this leads to a therapeutic position which views a parental fight as a natural consequence of the difficulty in managing shame and an event that provides therapists a welcomed opportunity to strengthen the parenting unit.

## 5.3 Responding to Different Levels of Shame in the Parents' Relationship

The higher the parent's shame level, the quicker the parents shift from a collaborative mode to an adversarial, hostile mode of interaction, both with the child and with each other. This refers to what I described as "loss of connection" (see Chap. 4). In the therapy room, the most typical signs that parents have lost their connection and shifted into an unregulated shame state include:

- Parents blaming each other for the child's problems: "You are too tough! You are too soft."
- Parents disagreeing on the actual definition of problematic behavior: "I think this is a problem!" "No, I think that is normal!"

[2] When I give workshops on parent training and ask participants in role-play activities to play a difficult family, they always choose parents who are fighting among themselves.

- Parents not listening to each other and only willing to hear the therapist.
- Parents attacking each other for being too involved or not being involved enough.

I also know that the parents are in an unregulated shame state by observing the parents' relationship with me[3]:

- One or both parents blame me for the child's behavior.
- One or both parents show resistance to interventions.
- Even when I am not directly attacked, I experience a "loss of empathy": I blame and become critical of one or both parents.

On the other hand, the regulated shame parent state manifests with the following signs:

- Parents can tolerate their differences; sometimes they can even see them as strengths.
- They use humor to explain the differences in their styles of parenting.
- Parents appreciate what the other parent is doing.
- Parents do not blame each other for the child's problem.
- Parents admit to their own roles in the fights with the child and want to approach the conflict differently.
- Parents can agree with some of the critique of their own parenting when the criticism is offered by the opposing parent.

Just as the unregulated shame state tends to affect the therapist, so does the regulated shame state. For example, when parents are in a regulated shame state, I notice that:

- I like the parents.
- I view the child's behavior, mainly, as a result of his own vulnerabilities and difficulties.
- The parents welcome my interventions and are interested in them.

When therapists witness parents shifting from a regulated shame state to an unregulated state, they should respond by shifting their own position. Otherwise, as observers of shaming interaction, they may easily lose their empathy and find themselves trapped in shaming dynamics with one or both parents. How do we discern that we are caught in a shaming dynamic with a parent? We notice that we are viewing the parent (or parents) in a negative way: blaming them for the child's problems and seeing them as egocentric, childish, impossible, and so forth. The three most common triggers for therapists to enter into such dynamics with parents are:

- Being unable to stop the parents from fighting with each other (the shame of feeling like a failure)

---

[3]One of the common complications of the parents' high shame state is that the therapist gets sucked into a high shame interaction with one or both parents. Once I am aware of that happening to me, I stop focusing on parenting issues and focus instead on repairing my relationship with the parents.

**Table 5.1** Therapist positioning in regulated and unregulated shame states

| | Parents in regulated shame state | Parents in unregulated shame state |
|---|---|---|
| Goal | Solving the problem | Solving the moment |
| Role of therapist | Expert | Translator |
| Flow of communication | Therapist to parents | Parent to parent |
| Coalitions | With parents as a team | With each parent individually |
| Time orientation | Future | Present |

- The parents resisting and not accepting the therapist's interventions (the shame of not being accepted, appreciated, or trusted by the parents)
- Being overtly blamed by one or both parents for either siding with the other parent or worsening/degrading their relationship with the child (the shame of failure and lack of acceptance plus the shame of the implied or stated accusation that the therapist lacks professional skills)

How do we prevent ourselves from being caught up in shame? It is by adjusting and shifting our own position to manage the unregulated shame state. This change in the therapeutic attitude is manifested in a number of important dimensions (see Table 5.1). These include:

*Goals* When parents are in a regulated shame state, the therapeutic goal is to "solve the problem." This means that therapists can comfortably enter into a problem-solving type of interaction with the parents; he/she can suggest new ways of approaching and relating to their child. Interventions are discussed and adjusted, and ultimately the therapist may lead the parents to try them out. However, when parents are in an unregulated shame state, the therapist can suggest the most creative parental interventions, only to have them rejected without much thought. In such states, the therapeutic goal is, what Dan Wile (2011) calls, "solving the moment." In solving the moment, the therapist tries to give words to unexpressed wishes, fears, or feelings that the parents cannot communicate to each other because they are experiencing so much shame. By doing so, the therapist overcomes the effects of shame and helps the parents to resume a more collaborative communication cycle.

*Role of the therapist* When parents are in a regulated shame state, the therapist's knowledge and expertise are welcomed and integrated with the parents' understanding. The regulated level of shame allows the parents to learn and to take the position of "students" without feeling humiliated about their status. However, once the therapist notices that the parents have entered an unregulated shame state, he or she needs to abandon the expert/authority role because it can easily add to the parents' shame. Instead, the therapist should embody the role of translator of each parents' experience. In these situations, what the parents need, more than anything else, are empathy and understanding of their subjective experience. Interestingly, when parents are in an unregulated shame state, they often want (and even put pressure on) the therapist to play the role of the expert and to decide "who is right and who is wrong." Accepting such a role when parents are in a high shame state often gets the therapist into trouble.

*Flow of communication* In regulated shame states, information is effectively and constructively exchanged between the therapist and the parents. In unregulated shame states, the flow of communication takes a different route and becomes focused on belligerent exchanges between the parents. In order to stop the parents from fighting, therapists often try to replace this communication flow with the one that resembles the regulated shame state, namely, talking to the parents and having the parents respond back. This strategy usually yields temporary relief from the fight, but it does not provide a solution to what evoked the unregulated shame dynamic in the first place.[4] In such situations I prefer to remain in the parent to parent communication flow and to translate each parent's position (using the systemic mirroring intervention described in Chap. 4). By doing so, I allow the needs, wishes, and fears of each parent to be heard and, ultimately, for shame to be regulated.

*Coalitions* Regulated shame states often feel like what Wile (1993) called "being on a platform," which means that the therapist and parents are able to view the problem from a united higher ground. They gain perspective, and both parents can see the problem without being drawn into it. At these moments, the ability to relate to both parents at the same time is both possible and welcomed by the parents. In contrast, unregulated shame states make simultaneously relating to both parents difficult. In such states, a more helpful strategy is to shift constantly between developing a separate coalition with each of the parents. Talking to both parents "as if" they were a team can increase both of the individuals' sense of isolation and sense of feeling misunderstood and ultimately lead to more shame in the system. Because the parents have lost their ability to feel connected to one another, they need to be connected to someone else first. They each need to have someone on their own side before they can resume their union as teammates.

*Time orientation* When parents are in a regulated shame state, the effective therapeutic position revolves around planning for the future: how, and with what approach, will the parents react when their child acts out. In unregulated shame states, the therapist should focus more on what is happening in the present: namely, the conflict between the parents. In doing so, parents receive tools that will enable them to deal with their future conflicts concerning their parental differences.

## 5.4 The Recovery of the Parental "Loss of Voice"

We have mentioned that escalating parental fights can be viewed as a sign of significant marital problems which endanger the parent training process. This is especially true when the therapist considers the goal of therapy to be "solving the problem" and his own role as that of the expert. In contrast, my approach is to view these fights as opportunities for regulating shame and as part of the development of the

[4] In working with divorced parents, this strategy is effective because there is no need to repair the intimate connection between the parents.

parental alliance. According to this view, parental fights are mostly a result of "loss of voice" – ineffective communication efforts which are really aimed at reducing one's shame but in this process transfer shame to the other parent. In such instances, the task of the therapist is to help parents recover from their "loss of voice." To do so, therapist's role should shift to that of a translator, transforming provocative statements into statements that capture the parent's full emotional experience. Common themes of translation include:

*Wanting recognition and respect* The often heard parental complaint "Our son never behaves that way when he's with me!" is typically interpreted as a way for one parent to berate and criticize the other. A more shame-sensitive position is to view this declaration as an ineffective effort to gain the respect of the other parent. Therefore, in such situations I intervene and say "I think that what your partner was trying to say to you is 'I don't mean to criticize you, but I wish you could see my success with our child and appreciate it'."

*A way of "making a point"* Parents use extreme statements in an attempt to communicate more effectively when an idea is of importance to them. This shame-based extremity comes at the expense of complexity; the messages come out one-dimensional and accusatory. In such situations, the parent needs someone who will help them to make the point without alienating the other parent. For example, if a father says to a mother "You don't know how to set boundaries! You let the children do whatever they want!," then I say to the mother "I think what your husband is trying to tell you is: 'I don't want to be angry with you, and I know that you care about our children, but I am really worried that if our child doesn't experience more boundaries his behavior will become worse'."

*Wanting a different type of teamwork* At the beginning of a parent training process, most parents are not working well as a team, but they have a hard time expressing it. Instead of saying "We are having a hard time cooperating with each other when we deal with our kids," they say "You always contradict what I do!" or "You always undermine my decisions!" What parents need is someone who will help them to turn these accusations into a conversation about co-parenting and/or turn these complaints into positive offers for a different approach to teamwork. For example, a response to the blaming message "You always do the opposite of what I do!" could be "O.k., what I hear your partner trying to tell you is: 'I know we have different styles in raising our children, but I wish we could find a better way to work as a team and thereby prevent generating all of this conflict between us'."

*Wanting to be able to talk more about the children* Other common complaints include "You are too tough!" or "You are too soft!" Differences in parental style are readily assumed to be the core cause of parental fights. Such complaints may lead a parent trainer to search for parental interventions which combine both soft and hard parental styles, thus allowing parents to work better as a team. This approach is often successful when shame is low (regulated) and the parental conflict is not too intense. When shame surpasses a certain level, such suggestions become less effective because they do not alleviate the problem at its source – shame. Moreover, differences in parental style are not necessarily what lead parents to fight, but, rather, it is their inability to relate to each other as having different styles that is at the heart of the conflict. It is the disrespect for the other's style, and the lack of savvy communication regarding the use of their differences as an advantageous co-parenting tool, that fuels parental fights. Based on this assumption, I like to use parental complaints as opportunities to improve the parents' ability to communicate with each other. I help them to talk about their diverse approaches to parenting in a way that will bring them closer to each other and foster intimacy rather than the rivalry of enemies. For example, I respond to the "too tough" or "too soft" criticisms with a statement such as "What I hear your partner trying to say is: 'I know we have different styles, but I wish that you would listen to my ideas about parenting without thinking that I just want to criticize you'."

## 5.5 Parental Team Building

Adjusting our therapeutic position to match the fluctuating shame state of the parents is very useful and yet can confuse or evoke anxiety in the parents. Shifting unexpectedly to meet the needs of unregulated shame states (a shift that is displayed by focusing on the parents' relationship with one another) can lead parents to protest and say "We didn't come here for couples therapy!"[5] Such objections can easily be prevented, if the therapist prepares the parents for such shifts. Consequently, in the first session, I ask permission from the parents to talk about their relationship as parents. I tell them explicitly that I have no intention of doing couple therapy with them, but that, instead, my goal is to turn them into the best team they can be. Then I ask them whether they want me to talk about and improve their teamwork as parents. Almost all parents respond positively to this therapeutic premise once they can make an informed choice to do so.

Positive recognition, communication, and teamwork turn each parent into the best parent that she or he can be. Yet, interventions for parents to utilize their relationship to empower each other have not been the focus of the parent training literature. This is unfortunate because each parent is in the best position to affect and improve the other parent's sense of being present for the child. Yet, when one parent is having a fight with the child, the other parent may find his or herself in a difficult dilemma; if the observing parent enters into the fight, they might lead the other parent to feel intruded upon, criticized, or that his or her judgment is not trusted. All of this increases the shame of the parent in conflict with the child. However, if the observing parent does not get involved, he or she might leave the other parent feeling ignored, abandoned, and resentful, which would increase their shame just as much.

When one parent is having a fight with the child, the other parent should assume the role of shame regulator for both of the fighting parties. Unfortunately, more often than not, the observing parent reacts in ways which just increase the shame in the

[5] This complaint is often raised by the father.

system. In order to clarify this process, let us first look at an example known to many of us: the drama of waking an adolescent up and having him get to school on time. For this example, I'll introduce a typical family. Yesterday evening, the parents, Thomas and Claire, had a talk with their 14-year-old son, Charlie, about waking up and getting to school on time. The mornings, the parents contended, have become impossible; they are a stream of constant fighting, with much yelling and anger. For Claire, the conversation was a very important one. As the sole parent who deals with Charlie's stubbornness every morning, her sense of success had come from *finally* being able to recruit her husband to take an active part in the conversation. Indeed, Thomas tried hard. He kept his composure (just like Claire had suggested), did not lose control (as Claire had suggested), and remained firm but fair (as Claire had suggested). The conversation ended with Charlie promising to wake up on time.

And now it is 7:00 in the morning, and Claire opens Charlie's bedroom door with optimism:

> "Charlie honey, good morning. It's 7:00 clock."

This is quite a dramatic moment for Claire. Let's imagine what would happen if Charlie were to immediately get out of bed:

- Claire would have a wonderful day at work.
- Claire would see herself as a competent mother.
- Claire would be happy that she and Thomas had the conversation with Charlie. She would feel that maybe she had been too harsh on him lately and that he was a good husband overall.
- Claire would feel confident about her own ability and her husband's ability to work as a good team.

But Charlie' answer is:

> "Just 5 more minutes ..."

Claire leaves the room, and at 7:10 she returns (a little worried). Seeing that Charlie has not yet woken up, and while still trying to remain calm and in control, she uses a voice that is a little more assertive:

> "Charlie, good morning, you have to get up."

And Charlie's response is:

> "I said 5 more minutes."

While Claire can feel her mounting irritation and anger, she is not aware of the shame building quickly inside of her. With every moment that passes, shame is intensifying because:

- She is feeling less and less powerful and more and more like a failure.
- She fears that her husband will say "I told you the conversation won't help, only punishments work."
- She had an expectation which is not being met.
- Charlie promised to wake up, and he is betraying her trust.

She decides to cool off and to give her son some space, but then at 7:18, hearing no sound of movement from his room, she decides to enter his room again:

> "Charlie! We agreed that you'd get up early. So come on! Get up immediately!"

And Charlie's answer:

> "Why do you always shout? I told you that I'm waking up."

Most fights between parents and children start as a fight between one of the parents and the child. Initially, the other parent is not involved in the conflict, which creates a discrepancy between the parents. As a result, one parent remains relatively safe (or emotionally stable), while the other parent becomes emotionally vulnerable. This is exactly what's happening with Claire. Although she is not aware of it, the longer the dispute drags on with Charlie, the greater the chance that her shame will take over. For this shame to be regulated, she needs someone to be on her side. While she would probably want her husband to join her in helping to wake Charlie up, on the emotional level, she needs much more than that. What she needs is someone who will ease the shame that she is experiencing. For example, she would probably appreciate:

- Getting a hug from her husband
- Her husband thanking her and acknowledging that she is doing all the hard work with their son
- Hearing that she is a good mom

Such actions will not get Charlie out of bed but will reduce Claire's shame. Fights with the child produce shame for the involved parent and generate an increasing wish that the other parent would make this shame go away.

Luckily for Claire (or so she thinks), Thomas just woke up and is about to enter the scene. Thomas finds himself in a very delicate situation regarding the regulation of shame in the family. His challenge is to try to do something that will, both, reduce his wife's shame and, at the same time, not increase his son's shame. This is no easy task and, unfortunately, Thomas had only slept for a few hours. He is now tired, and the yelling between the mother and son woke him up. He quickly enters Charlie's room and shouts:

> "Tell me, why can't you just get up and get ready like your sister!? Why do I have to be woken up every morning by you and your mother shouting!? I've really had enough of you! Until further notice, there's no TV and no computer for you!!"

The father's reflexive and misguided intervention actually served to *increase* the shame of both the mother and the son; soon even Thomas will feel shame over his own behavior. While the parents did manage to work well as a team in a cool situation (during the talk with Charlie), they lost this capacity once they had to work as a team in real time, and when emotions spontaneously flared. That is exactly the point in time when most parents do not know how to make good use of their relationship.

## 5.6 Parents Helping Each Other Shift Out of High Shame States

The first moment, in which the observing parent reaches out to the parent who just had a fight with the child, is a moment with enormous potential for increasing that parent's experience of being valued and appreciated and feeling connected. Knowing that, I like to prepare parents for such moments.

During fights, parents forget who they are. This inability to access and utilize knowledge that they already possess is one of the paralyzing effects of shame which I termed "loss of voice." The intensity of the shame creates splits within the self, which distort one's view of self, as well as one's view of the other. We need someone to remind us of who we are, what we are really fighting for, what we believe in, our strengths, and our values. In working with parents, my goal is to facilitate a relationship between them, so that they can remind each other of these truths (see Table 5.2). I want to help the parents to talk about their parenting in a way that strengthens their presence as parents and provides for intimate moments as a couple. I do that by helping them learn how to shift, in real time, from a high shame parent state to a low shame parent state and, more specifically, how each one of them can regulate the other's shame.

In the next section, I show how different parental interactions can facilitate that regulation. Each short excerpt demonstrates how the parental dialogue, which could turn into a fight (or a "loss of connection"), instead turns into a collaborative interaction, which provides regulation for the parent who was experiencing intense shame.

### *5.6.1 Regulating Shame by Reminding the Parent of His or Her Values*

In the first example, the mother approaches the father right after he'd had a loud fight with the son. Both father and son had screamed, yelled, and said hurtful words to each other.

Father – I feel like killing him!
Mother – Well, he sure knows how to press all the buttons.
Father – Yes, but I lost control and said things I should never have said!
Mother – Maybe, but in my view, you are still a good dad.

*Initially, the father is angry at the child. If the mother had been having a bad day herself, she might have responded with statements such as "Why do you always have to fight with him!" or "Why can't you control yourself? You are the adult! You are the father!" Such statements would have reflected her own loss of empathy as an observer. But today the mother is at her best, and she is aware of her role in regulating her husband's shame. Instead of blaming the father, she responds by,*

**Table 5.2** Reminders that help parents regulate their shame

| Values | Influence | Togetherness |
|---|---|---|
| "I respect your values as a parent" | "You have influence" | "You are not alone" |
| "Your actions are the result of your deep beliefs" | "What you do matters" | "I see what you do and appreciate it" |

*first, legitimizing his anger. This creates a shift within the father and helps him to see that he is really angry at himself for having behaved in ways which do not match his values. As a result, he feels guilt instead of shame.*[6] *Mother shows understanding for his loss of control and reminds him that he is a good father.*

Father – A good dad doesn't call his son a "stupid idiot"!

*This statement could shift the parents' interaction into an adversarial one. The mother has already shown plenty of patience and might have had enough of the father's complaints. If she were to evaluate her own attempts to regulate her husband's shame as having failed, she would start experiencing her own shame, leading her to say something like "You're right; don't ever say such a thing again!" But the mother is still in a regulated shame state and, instead, reassures the father:*

Mother – He said some awful things, himself, and provoked you; at the same time, I know that you hate losing control; it's not your style.
Father –You're right. I hate being like that; it's just not me.
Mother – And you care about him, and you're worried about him.
Father – I should let him know that without losing control and exploding!
Mother – With our son, it's really hard to be a Buddha. I lose control with him, you lose control, and he definitely loses control. If you feel that you need to apologize for your actions, we can do that.
Father –Yes, that's what I will do.

*The mother communicates to the father that, in her eyes, he is still a good father. By doing so, she is regulating the father's shame. This leads to a pragmatic course of action, which helps the father to behave in ways which he, himself, views as worthy and fair. Finding a way to act in accord with his values repairs the father's sense of being "bad" and allows him to develop empathy for his son. If the mother had suggested to the father that he apologize, without that whole prior regulation process, he would probably have dismissed it and become angry at her.*

[6]In this book, I have not elaborated on the differences between guilt and shame but in a nutshell: guilt is specific to a behavior (I have done a bad thing) and leads to acts of repairing (contrition). Shame is much more global (I am bad) and most commonly leads to attacking the other or attacking the self (Tangney and Dearing 2002).

### 5.6.2 *Regulating Shame by Reminding the Parent of His or Her Influence*

The mother approaches the father after he'd had a fight with the son concerning Friday night curfew.[7]

Mother –Thanks for taking care of that.
Father – But he didn't listen to me at all, and I don't know why I always have to be the one to take care of it!

*Although the mother came with good intentions, the father is still angry and emotionally aroused from the fight with the child. He responds to the mother's positive statement by attacking her. This can easily lead to a mutual shaming interaction between the parents. However, the mother continues in a collaborative tone:*

Mother – He listened to you more than he would have listened to me. If I had been there, things would have gotten worse.

*The mother is doing something remarkable here. She shows the father that he has influence over the child. She lets the father know that she does not see his efforts as futile and meaningless but rather that she sees them as positive and constructive.*

Father – I guess you're right.
Mother – With all his arguing, you still have some impact on him. I wish I had that.
Father – You're right; he does listen to me sometimes.

*In two sentences, the mother helps the father to regain his sense of competence and self-esteem. She focuses on his successes and not on his failures. This helps the father to experience a sense of his own influence and power, leading to a reduction in shame, and even to a sense of pride.*

### 5.6.3 *Regulating Shame by Moving Closer, Appreciating, and Experiencing Togetherness*

In this example, the father approaches the mother after she has helped their daughter with her homework:

Father – Thanks for helping Maya with her homework.
Mother – Well, someone has to do it!

[7]The second example is another example in which the mother regulates the father's shame. I have no intention of suggesting that this is the mother's role, more than it is the father's. In the next example, it will be the father regulating the mother's shame.

*Although the father is trying to communicate recognition, the mother is experiencing his statement as implying that helping the daughter with her homework will always be the mother's duty. She experiences his thanks as patronizing and responds by attacking. This could easily lead to a shaming dynamic (*e.g., *father responding with "You're wrong; I do a lot of homework with Maya!," or "Stop playing the martyr!"). However, today the father is aware of his role in regulating shame, and instead, he continues with a collaborative tone*:

Father – I know, and I wanted to let you know that I notice what you do, and that I appreciate it.
Mother – You do?

*Mother is not used to father communicating in such a way and is reacting with disbelief. However, she has already softened up.*

Father – I probably should tell you this more often, and not let you feel that it's solely your responsibility.
Mother – It's not such a big deal, but I appreciate you saying that.

*Only a few minutes ago, the mother felt frustrated and alone. The father's words let her feel that she is valued by him, seen by him, and cared for by him. His appreciation and recognition help her to feel that helping Maya is "not such a big deal."*

Can parents speak this way to each other? Yes, but only if one of them remains in a regulated shame state. If they try to force themselves to speak in this manner when they are really experiencing an unregulated shame state, it will come off as false and insincere and be ineffective. In parenting, unregulated shame states are easy to fall into. In my work with parents, I help them to shift from such states which are characterized by attacking, blaming, and criticizing behaviors to regulated shame states, which are characterized by a collaborative dynamic. I explain to parents that their freedom is not manifested in whether they will experience shame or not but, rather, in whether they will have the power to move closer to one another once the shame reaction has already forced them apart.

## References


Belsky, J., Putnam, S., & Crnic, K. (1996). Coparenting, parenting, and early emotional development. *New Directions for Child and Adolescent Development, 1996*(74), 45–55.

Brown, B. (2015). *Daring greatly: How the courage to be vulnerable transforms the way we live, love, parent, and lead*. New York: Penguin.

Feinberg, M. E. (2003). The internal structure and ecological context of coparenting: A framework for research and intervention. *Parenting: Science and Practice, 3*(2), 95–131.

Konold, T. R., & Abidin, R. R. (2001). Parenting alliance: A multifactor perspective. *Assessment, 8*(1), 47–65.

McHale, J. P., Kuersten-Hogan, R., & Rao, N. (2004). Growing points for coparenting theory and research. *Journal of Adult Development, 11*(3), 221–234.

Miller, S. (1985). *The shame experience*. Hillsdale, NJ: Erlbaum.

Pattison, S. (2000). *Shame: Theory, therapy, theology*. Cambridge University Press.

Tangney, J. P., & Dearing, R. L. (2002). Shame and guilt. New York, NY: Guilford Press.

Weinblatt, U. (2013). Die Kraft der zwei Anker: Wie die Beziehung der Eltern ihre Präsenz und Autorität stärkt (The power of two anchors: How the parents' relationship can strengthen their presence and authority). In M. Grabbe, J. Borke, & C. Tsirigotis (Eds.), *Autorität, Autonomie und Bindung: Die Ankerfunktion bei elterlicher und professioneller Präsenz* (pp. 85–100). Göttingen: Vandenhoeck & Ruprecht.

Weissman, S. H., & Cohen, R. S. (1985). The parenting alliance and adolescence. *Adolescent Psychiatry, 12*, 24–45.

Wile, D. B. (1993). *After the fight: Using your disagreements to build a stronger relationship*. New York: Guilford Press.

Wile, D. B. (2011). Collaborative couple therapy: Turning fights into intimate conversations. *Psychotherapy in Australia, 17*(3), 52.

# Chapter 6
# Regulating Intense Shame of Noncooperative Adolescents: When Dialogue Breaks Down

When shame surpasses a certain threshold, the ability to collaborate with others comes to a halt. For adolescents who experience high levels of shame, such situations are common. These teens often display various problems including self-cutting, school refusal, aggression, drug abuse, and other dysfunctional behaviors. They persistently refuse to admit to having a problem and refuse to accept help. This attitude often leaves their parents, teachers, and therapists in states of helplessness, anger, and anxiety because they don't know how to move the child forward, when the main path towards progress, verbal communication, is often unavailable, blocked, and even forbidden.

## 6.1 The Effects of Intense Shame

When people experience shame for too long or too intensely, they desperately try to avoid or eliminate any situation which might arouse the feeling again. As they distance themselves from shame, they seem to behave as if they have no shame. Meanwhile, in the face of the slightest shame provoking interaction (any demand from another person, any remark, comment, or suggestion), the person will either act out and attack (Gilligan 2001; Potter-Efron 2007), or leave the situation and try to avoid it altogether. This process leads to continual disruptions in relationships and to an inability to communicate authentically. Ultimately, it leads to the breakdown of dialogue and turns verbal communication efforts into frustrating and dangerous encounters. In such situations, people who are close to the shame-ridden person (family members, teachers, friends) feel they must walk on eggshells, knowing very well that talking freely can lead to intense escalations. It is exactly in these situations that collaborative-/communication-oriented relational gestures reach their limit.



U. Weinblatt, *Shame Regulation Therapy for Families*,
https://doi.org/10.1007/978-3-319-77470-1_6

Intense shame does not allow for cooperation. The person experiencing such shame cannot cooperate because he or she feels that cooperating will increase their shame. In such circumstances, cooperating with others feels like giving in, a humiliation, or even morally wrong. In addition, intense shame significantly reduces the ability of the person to feel empathy (Tangney and Dearing 2002; Tangney et al. 2007) and therefore reduces his ability to communicate effectively. As the person's capacity to cooperate deteriorates, the relational bridge that connects him to others breaks down, leaving the person alone and humiliated.

For adolescents, the effects of intense shame ricochet through life's spheres like wounding bullets:

### 6.1.1 On the Individual Level

The adolescent experiences an incapacitating "loss of voice" – an inability to express his[1] thoughts and feelings, both to others and to himself. The teen will often respond with "I don't know" to a range of questions, blame others "It's your fault!", or blame himself "I told you I am a fuckup!" Often, the only emotion expressed is anger. When anger is absent, a determined refusal to talk replaces it.

### 6.1.2 On the Relationship Level

The presence of intense shame leads to a "loss of connection" and diminishes the ability of the adolescent and his parents (or other adults) to have collaborative and constructive interactions or to share enough positive experiences. There is no "real talk," just emotionally shallow exchanges. The default mode of the relationship is distant and adversarial, occasionally punctuated with devastating outbursts (by either child or parent), which further damage the relationship. Simultaneously, pleasurable joint activities cease. Without such positive and shame-reducing interactions, the parent-child relationship becomes one which revolves entirely around problems, thus leading to more and more shame. As the capacity of the shamed child[2] to cooperate drops further, the parents' level of helplessness, anger, and, ultimately, shame increases. These processes lead to a gradual rise in the dynamics of paralysis; the adolescent and his parents are caught in a trap of shame, in which their reactions, both attacking and disconnecting, only intensify each other's feelings of failure, inferiority, and disgust.

[1] For the sake of literary fluency, I will often refer to hypothetical adolescents as male, but the reader should keep in mind that this adolescent could be of any gender.

[2] This chapter focuses on noncooperative adolescents, although the model presented has also been utilized in working with younger children as well as adults.

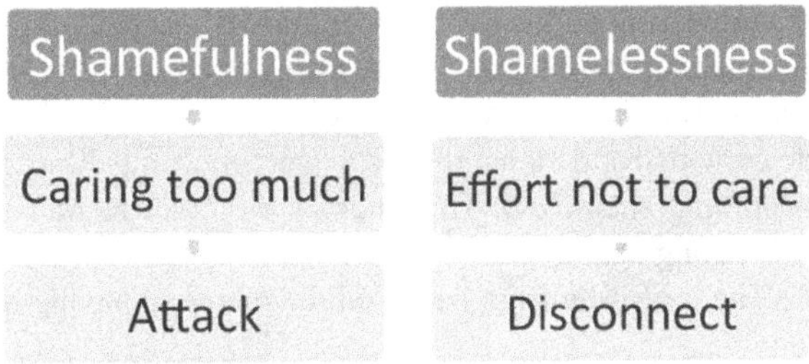


**Fig. 6.1** Shameful and shameless states

### *6.1.3 On the Observer/Group Level*

As the noncooperative behaviors escalate and become more public, the patience of those who are connected to the family erodes, and a "loss of empathy" is experienced by anyone observing the adolescent's behavior. Soon, the presence of others is not perceived as a resource, but rather as a source of additional shame. The processes of social stigmatization create a snowball effect, leading the adolescent and his family to become more disconnected from their social milieu. In such situations, families tend to involve fewer people in their affairs and become more isolated. Yet, this isolation can easily lead parents and teens to feel worse because they lose the opportunity for others to ease their shame.

## 6.2 Shameful or Shameless?

One of the key problems in addressing intense shame states is that they do not resemble shame in the way that we expect to see it. The physical manifestations of shame – covering the face, lowering the eyes, and blushing – are absent. Instead, we observe behaviors we associate with rage or apathy. These kids seem disconnected from shame, or simply shameless; they often treat others without respect and generally behave in ways that shame others:

Mother: "He screamed and yelled and then broke my favorite china plates that were given to me by my mother."
Therapist: "And afterwards, did he apologize?"
Mother: "Exactly the opposite. He said it was my fault; he blamed me!"

Does this example show behavior that is a consequence of experiencing too much shame, or too little shame? The question is important because the process of regulating intense shame conditions demands the ability to differentiate between two opposing yet related states: the state of shamefulness and the state of shamelessness (see Fig. 6.1).

Shamefulness is an outcome of caring too much. In such states, shame is experienced as humiliation, disappointment, vulnerability, and pain and often leads to rage or attacking the other. Shamelessness, on the other hand, is the outcome of the effort to stop caring and is experienced mostly as apathy, disconnection, and withdrawal. In situations of intense shame, the adolescent shifts intermittently between the two states. The intensely shameful reaction creates debilitating pain which can only be dealt with by distancing, disconnecting, and dissociating from it, or simply by becoming shameless. This enables the child to transcend his vulnerability and to feel strong again.

The transition from being full of shame to having no shame is often confusing:

Parent: "I don't know what happened to her. I just told her that she needs to do her homework, and suddenly, she started yelling and cursing at me. Later, she approached me as if nothing happened."
Therapist: "Was it as if she initially overreacted, and then later seemed not to care at all?"
Parent: "Yes, exactly!"

Such shifts are common in teens who have a poor ability to regulate shame. Let's look at a variation of this dynamic:

Parent: "He behaved terribly. I brought him a tutor to help him with his homework, and suddenly he went into such a rage. It was really awful. I thought he might hurt me or himself."
Therapist: "And what happened later?"
Parent: "After a few hours, he cooled down and acted as if nothing had happened."
Therapist: "And how did that affect you?"
Parent: "I don't know what to make of it. I just don't understand him."

Of course, the parents are not the only ones to be confused. Often, the adolescent, himself, does not know how to explain such emotional outbursts. It is then no wonder that, when asked, they frequently answer with "don't know."

## 6.3 The Fundamentals of Regulating Intense Shame

Since most teens who experience intense shame refuse to enter therapy (or when they do, they can't make it meaningful), the process of change is usually led by the parents (and/or school personnel). Steering the regulation process is tricky, for it demands two opposing actions:

- Reintroducing/exposing shame when it is absent (in states of shamelessness)
- Reducing the adolescent's shame when it is experienced too painfully (in states of shamefulness)

When shame is unfelt and absent, the goal is to integrate it back into the teen's life. Since the ability to tolerate shame is a result of experiencing it in levels that enable mastery, we induce shame in ways that allow the child to manage it and that ultimately lead to the positive outcome of shame – knowing one's limits.

**Table 6.1** Interventions for treating intense shame/noncooperative states

| | Shamefullness state | Shamelessness state |
|---|---|---|
| Parental interventions | Deshaming communication | Sitting with shame |
| Supporters/Third siders interventions | Collective mirroring | Systemic exposure |

The exposure to shame is never welcomed by the teen and evokes intense reactions. The two main interventions that assist in achieving these goals are "systemic exposure" and "sitting with shame."

When shame is too strong, the goal is to ease the pain. We do so by reconnecting with the child, even if he forbids and opposes it. The two main interventions used to accomplish this are "collective mirroring" and "deshaming communication."

The four shame regulatory interventions – systemic exposure, sitting with shame, deshaming communication, and collective mirroring – are all based on interventions used in the nonviolent resistance (NVR) parent training program (Omer 2004). One of the main strengths of this model is that it doesn't demand any cooperation from the child in order to be successful. This lack of dependency on the child's motivation enables parents (and teachers) to move forward, act, and lead change without being in the frustrating position of awaiting the child's acceptance of help. The rest of this chapter is devoted to describing the four interventions. This chapter is written in a different style than that of the other chapters in this book. They make more use of dialogue and verbal transactions. The difference is not coincidental. In noncooperative states, the power of dialogue to regulate shame shrinks. Instead, for change to occur, one must take action (Table 6.1).

## 6.4 Systemic Exposure

When shame is intense, behaviors of "hiding" are always prevalent. The adolescent hides because he is ashamed of his failures (often social and academic in nature), ashamed of his own destructive behaviors, even ashamed of existing. The parents hide because they are ashamed of their parenting, of their child's behavior, of needing help, and of their helplessness. Thus, both adolescent and parent are heavily invested in maintaining a distance from one another and from others, as their presence puts them in danger of feeling more shame.

Shame is triggered by feeling overexposed and by feeling evaluated in a critical way by others (Smith et al. 2002). It is an experience of having no control over how we are being seen and what we allow others to see in us. While behaviors such as disconnecting, hiding, and concealing seem, at first, to protect the adolescent (and the parents) from the judgmental eye of others, they do not enable him or her to connect with others, which is ultimately the best cure for shame. In fact, it is the hiding and isolation that maintain the problem and intensify the shame response. This occurs for a number of reasons:

First, secrecy enables problems to continue and escalate. Without the presence of the public eye, there are fewer obstacles, fewer boundaries, and fewer inhibitions for the continuation of the dysfunctional behavior (Jacquet 2015).

Second, avoiding shame increases sensitivity to shame and does not enable the person to learn how to tolerate and regulate it. As a result, the passage of time makes the person become more fearful and sensitive to experiencing shame.

Finally (and this is what makes shame so unique and painful), even when we are hiding from others, we can never hide from our own inner critical audience that continues the shaming process (Tangney et al. 1996; Wurmser 2000). This inner audience is often more judgmental, critical, and stigmatizing than most "real" people. Without the stabilizing effects of real supportive others, the person is left alone to face the harsh inner voices that never tire of reminding him just how awful, disgusting, and bad he is.

To regulate intense shame, other people (whether family members, friends, or school personnel) must be involved. The ability to speak out, and to turn that which is secretive into a public affair, is fundamental to the process of empowerment and emancipation from shame (Sanderson 2015; Shapiro and Powers 2011).

### *6.4.1 Renegotiating What Is Private and What Is Public*

Shame draws the line between what may be spoken of and what should be shrouded in silence. When shame is unregulated, privacy and secrecy reign. It is usually the level of shame that constructs and signifies the boundary between what is private and what can become public. As shame levels rise, private life becomes more dominant, and outsiders are kept at a distance that prevents them from knowing the family well. When the level of shame continues to increase, the opinions of others become threatening and dangerous. This process breeds increasing levels of alienation, isolation, and more shame, which in turn present more obstacles that discourage people from utilizing their support systems in helpful ways.

In the systemic exposure intervention, shame is regulated by renegotiating the boundaries between what is private and what is public. The parents are coached to openly tell the adolescent that they are planning on involving other people "who care about our family and are willing to help us move forward." This statement is not intended to be a threat ("if you won't behave we will tell …") but a new parental position that is challenging the effects of shame and that welcomes the intervention of others. Parents are instructed to disclose the behaviors of the child that were considered taboo (aggressive behaviors, substance abuse, isolation, etc.) and to request that these newly informed supporters contact the adolescent. This process is not easy; it demands that the parents overcome a number of obstacles that are all related to the danger of being shamed by others. These include:

- *The shame of needing help*. In our individualistic and independent culture, needing help is shameful. Needing help and not receiving it is even worse. Parents often fear that their request for help from others will be denied and rejected.
- *The shame of failing*. There is no guarantee that involving others will change the dynamic between parent and child. Parents who are already experiencing a sense of defeat do not need another failure in their lives, as that would shame them further.
- *Stigma*. Parents feel that going public would potentially stigmatize the child and would lead others to reject him. They are also worried about being stigmatized, themselves, as bad, weak, or incompetent parents.

In preparation for involving others, parent's concerns regarding the possibility of being shamed are validated and discussed. To minimize these risks, the exposure intervention is carefully planned. This leads to a controllable exposure experience, maximizing the potential of the group for management of shame, while reducing the negative shaming processes.

Two groups of family experiences that tend to be swept under the rug during intense family conflicts are exposed. The first is harmful behaviors (violence, self-harm) that are related to intense shame or humiliations of different sorts. The second group of experiences which get overlooked is the positive behaviors of the child, such as improved functioning in school and in other arenas, acts of kindness towards the parents or siblings, and respectful behaviors of various kinds.

The messages that others are requested to deliver to the child (via SMS, phone, email, and letters) are short, concise, and composed of three parts: knowing, evaluation, and a deshaming statement. Knowing and evaluation evoke shame, while the deshaming statement regulates it. For example, a message delivered to an adolescent boy (after an incident in which he hit his mother) can take the following form:

- Knowing – "I know that you hit your mother last night."
- Evaluation – "I think that it's wrong to hit her."
- Deshaming – "I care about you and your family, and I still think that you are a good person. Let me know if I can help."

Such messages have been found to be very effective in reducing a wide range of aggressive and disrespectful behaviors (Weinblatt and Omer 2008). The response from the public provides perspective and balance: the child receives a message in which the shameful incident is seen by the public as situational and doesn't infer anything global about who he is. For adolescents who experience too little shame, the involvement of the public raises the teen's level of shame to the threshold where shame's original healthy function (inhibiting hurtful behaviors towards others) is actualized.

While the systemic exposure intervention initially increases the level of shame by countering the shamelessness strategy, it ultimately leads to an improved capacity to regulate shame. This is similar to one's capability of tolerating more anxiety as a result of being exposed to it. However, what makes the systemic exposure so powerful is that it reintroduces other people into the adolescent's life in an authentic way. This resembles what Braithwaite (1989) calls "reintegrative shaming," a process of justice seeking in which shaming is followed by efforts to reintegrate the offender back into the community (Ahmed et al. 2001). Thus, not only is the adolescent exposed to shame, but he also experiences the healing effect of belonging. This is exactly the opposite process of stigmatization, which implies a disintegrative shaming process in which the adolescent is publically humiliated and others distance themselves from him.

Messages that amplify and congratulate good behavior are also part of the systemic exposure intervention and are delivered in the same way. Such messages are effective because adolescents experiencing intense shame tend to forbid their parents to share the teen's accomplishments, success, or anything positive about them with others. For example, a boy who used to physically hit his sister received this message after a good day with her:

- Knowing – "I know that you invested time with your sister and were kind to her."
- Opinion – "I really appreciate you for doing that."
- Deshaming – "I hope it's ok that I am writing this to you. I was just happy when I heard about it."

Sending messages of both types maximizes the potential for regulation by others. Exposing "the good, the bad, and the ugly" evokes a shame response, but does so in a controlled way. Interestingly, such messages do not push the child into an intensely shameful position that would lead him to become aggressive and retaliate (as many parents fear it will). What occurs is just the opposite. Adolescents who experience such exposure become more regulated, and their motivation to change grows.

## 6.5 Sitting with Shame: Challenging Noncooperative States

For shame to be regulated, it needs to be exposed. Yet the more intense the shame is, the less chance the adolescent will be willing to face his difficulties. Furthermore, the adolescent will behave in ways which are more provocative and seem shameless, for example:

- Being caught stealing and not caring about it
- Screaming so loud at parents that the neighbors start banging on the walls
- Being violent (verbally or physically) and not showing remorse
- Breaking things at home
- Not going to school and not caring about it
- Behaving in different provocative and self-entitled ways

As with other intense shame behaviors, the problem is not only the destructive nature of these behaviors. There is also an inability to enter into any constructive dialogue in order to reduce these behaviors, the adults are unable to elicit any kind of reaction from the adolescent that transcends the common behaviors of attacking or disconnecting.

A second major intervention for regulating these kinds of shameless states is the "sitting with shame" intervention. It is based on an intervention called the "sit-in" which was developed by Haim Omer (2001) and later systemized in the nonviolent resistance (NVR) program (Omer et al. 2004). The intervention provides a unique approach to exposing parent and child to shame in a process through which both sides learn to cope with, tolerate, and, ultimately, better regulate it. To maximize its potential for regulating shame states, I expanded the intervention to accommodate shame-related processes. Just like the original sit-in, sitting with shame does not demand the collaboration of the adolescent in order to be successful. As such, it is of crucial importance when coaching parents of adolescents with high levels of shame and low levels of cooperation.

The intervention consists of the parents entering and sitting in the adolescent's room (when he is there) for a period of up to 45 minutes. The parents are coached to enter the adolescent's room and to sit on the floor next to the child's door. As they enter the room, they can use one of the following statements:

"We are here because we are very worried about your safety. We love you and you are important to us. We will sit here in order to find out how we can move forward."

"I'm sorry to bother you, but I have something to say that has been on my mind..."

"I want us both to sit and think about what happened yesterday, and to think about what we can each do differently."

The goal of the intervention is to challenge the adolescent's shameless/noncooperative disposition and, at the same time, to improve the parents' ability to regulate their own shame. This is done through two processes:

### 6.5.1 Exposure to Shame

1. The parents entering and staying in the adolescent's room creates a discontinuation of a pleasurable activity for him. Tomkins (1963) has suggested that it is exactly these types of activating behaviors that lead to the shame response.
2. The parents enter the child's room without his permission. As such, they are renegotiating the boundaries of what is private. This intrusion evokes shame because the adolescent feels that what had previously been considered private has now been turned into a public domain.

The parents put the spotlight on a behavior that the adolescent feels ashamed of. Whether it is low school performance, isolation, aggressive behaviors, eating disorders, self-inflicted injury, lack of safe sexual boundaries, cyber bullying, or drug use, they bring up an issue in the adolescent's life that feels to him/her like a failure. Exposing this failure intensifies the shame reaction.

### 6.5.2 Regulation of Shame

Through the parents' consistent actions for containing and managing the child's under-regulated shame, the adolescent develops better regulation capacities. During this process, adolescent reactions oscillate between attacking and disconnecting behaviors which include:

*Demanding that the parents leave, or physically trying to leave* The first reaction of the adolescent is either to try and leave the room or to try to get the parents out. In such situations, the parents are instructed to remain in the room and resist leaving. Only if the adolescent becomes violent should they leave the room (in such cases parents are instructed that future interventions will include additional people. The presence of these supporters reduces dramatically the chances of violent behaviors). If the adolescent has left the room, the parents can follow him quietly, saying "We don't want to upset you or hurt you, but we need to talk." They should then remain in proximity to him for the rest of the time scheduled, even if he is not in his room. In cases where the adolescent leaves the home, the parents may follow him, or later find out where he is staying and approach the place (a friend's house). They should let him know that they are outside the house waiting for him.

*Trying to distract themselves* Another common reaction is trying to avoid the situation through distraction. The adolescent will look at his smart phone, get into bed, play music, turn on his computer, or find anything that can shift his attention from the parental request. The parents are instructed to ask the child once to stop these activities. If the child continues (as they often do), the parents are instructed to remain in the room for the planned time. The best way to handle the avoidant/disconnected shame reaction is to maintain their position and let time make the real impact. As time passes, the parents are instructed to physically move closer to the child (often only one parent). They can also use encouraging statements, such as "We can make this better," "We know this is not easy," and "Everything is going to be ok." Our experience shows that the parents' presence combined with these deshaming statements is a powerful tool in regulating the adolescent's shame.

*Attacking the parents (verbally)* For some adolescents, the exposure to shame will result in their immediate shift to a shameful state. Feeling the pain of shame, they attack the parents in different ways. This often takes the form of name calling, screaming, and trying to ridicule the parents with deliberate humiliation. In these moments, it is important that the parents maintain their self-control and respond minimally, often lowering their eyes in order to not provoke more shame. The most effective reaction in this phase is to remain quiet. Parents can say, "We respect you and don't want to hurt you," yet, often, any words will lead to a powerful retaliation, and the wisest approach is to remain quiet and wait it out.

*Attacking through ignoring* This reaction resembles that of disconnecting through distracting. The teen refuses to get into any dialogue and, instead, plays on one of his electronic devices and gets into bed or any other ignoring behavior. The difference here is the intention. The adolescent is trying to transfer the shame back to the parents, communicating with his actions the message "I am stronger than you," "You are not important," and "I don't give a shit about what you want." As with the former attacking reaction, it is the ability of the parents to manage their own shame that allows them to cope successfully with the adolescent in this state. The parents can use a (minimally) deshaming statement such as "We don't want to hurt you," "We care about you," "You are important," and wait. However, it is time and quietness that help the adolescent to shift from this state, and therefore, the parents should refrain from filling the room with too much verbiage at this stage.

*The beginning of a conversation* After the attacking and distancing behaviors have been used up, the adolescent will make his first effort to have a conversation. Since, in this phase, his level of shame is not regulated, he will be highly ambivalent and there will be a big part of him that doesn't want to converse and will try to sabotage it. At this stage the parents are instructed to remain humble in their goals, meaning that they do not make too much of an effort to develop a conversation. Trying too much often backfires; it leads back to attacking behaviors. Therefore, when the adolescent asks, "What do you want from me?", or says "Why are you doing this to me?" or "Who gave you this stupid idea?", the parents should repeat what they initially had said. If the teen does not attack them for saying so, then they can add "We are curious to hear your thoughts about that."

*A fuller conversation* These usually do not follow when the teen is in an intensely noncooperative state. If they do, the parents are coached to avoid centering the conversation on problem solving. Rather, the conversation should focus on how the parents felt and how the teen felt. Any move in the direction of problem solving will lead to unnecessary escalation. The goal of this conversation is to "give voice" to both adolescent and parent while maintaining a connection.

Naturally, adolescents do not like this intervention. They feel ganged-up on, controlled, and pressured. They are "forced" into experiencing shame, an emotion they fear and try to avoid. However, in the period after the intervention, parents often observe the adolescent's range of behaviors and emotions increasing, becoming richer and more nuanced. When successful, "sitting with shame" results in the following outcomes:

- The adolescent can tolerate the shame of his parents being "above him," or simply taking a parenting role in his life.
- The adolescent can better tolerate the feeling of "having a problem" and "needing help." Issues which were considered taboo can be discussed.
- The adolescent spends more time with his parents, will tolerate their presence in his room, and will tend to engage more during family rituals.
- The parents can tolerate the shame of the adolescent's various humiliating behaviors; they do not react as quickly and as harshly to shaming messages from the teen.
- The parents feel that they have more empathy towards their child. Parents feel that they "see" their child in a different way.

The adolescent, then, is not the sole benefiter of this intervention. Parents also change, learning that they can emancipate themselves from their patterned shame reactions to the child's attack/withdraw shame behaviors. In their daily lives, the parents may still fluctuate between shame-triggered, explosive/rigid reactions and withdrawing/disconnecting responses, but "sitting with shame" provides them with an experience of having successfully done something different that transcends their typical reactions to shame.

For parents who felt helpless and afraid of their adolescent, seeing change in their child's behavior is a dramatic experience. It cultivates hope, re-motivates the parents, and lets them experience themselves as parents with influence. I always wish for parents to have such an experience. However, immediate change in the child's behavior is not the only criteria for evaluating success; it's not even the main criteria. Many of the families I treat have been dealing with behavioral issues for years. There is no one intervention that can make all that go away. The expectation for immediate change can lead both parents and therapist to experience disappointment, despair, and more shame.

## 6.6 Collective Mirroring: Countering the Third Siders' (Observers) Loss of Empathy

A major problem for the person experiencing shame, and for his family, is that they lose the empathy of others who are connected to them. By "others" I mean any third party who witnesses the behaviors of the shamed person and the person interacting with him.

Indeed, it is difficult to be nonjudgmental when a person is angry, accusative, and avoidant, bullies, or expresses contempt towards another person:

Mother (addresses son after a family dinner): "John, would you please pick up the dishes?"
Son: "Why should I?"
Mother: "Can you please lower your voice? Your grandparents don't need to hear all this!"
Son: "Why, they should know what kind of mother you are!"
Grandfather (getting angry at grandson): "I don't like the way you are speaking to your mother!"
John: "I don't care!" (Storms out of the room)
Grandfather (to mother): "He is so disrespectful."
Mother: "Please Dad, not another lecture about how I should be tougher on him!"

When others lose their ability to have empathy for the adolescent (and his family), they can quickly turn into a powerful shaming device. In such situations the community can amplify negative interactions that intensify escalation processes, leading to stigmatization and ostracism.

In order to regulate the shame that is constantly fed by their adversarial relationship, both parents and adolescent need acceptance and recognition from others. Yet more often than not, the parents and the child receive criticism when they need approval. This is particularly evident when observing helpless parents of shame suffering adolescents. These parents are often shamed by their partner, school staff, and other adults from their social networks. This does not help, for both adolescent and parent delegitimize themselves, feeling inadequate, unworthy, and full of self-blame.

### 6.6.1 From Criticism to Empathy

The power of the family's social support system to improve parental and adolescent functioning has been repeatedly demonstrated (Armstrong et al. 2005). I believe that the impact of family supporters is largely a result of their ability to regulate the shame of all family members. Supporters can help parents regain control over their own behaviors, change their attitudes towards their children, and help to restore communication between parent and teen. Moreover, strong support systems have the ability to change the shame-based negative belief systems and aggressive/critical behaviors of, both, parents and adolescents.

While the initial goal of "systemic exposure" intervention is to raise the shame level of the adolescent, "collective mirroring" aims to reduce the shame level of the adolescent. The shame regulatory functions of collective mirroring include reparation and reconciliation. In healthy relationships, the more powerful family member usually administers reparation "first-aid" in order to regulate shame. A similar dynamic has also been observed in primates, where, after a fight, it can be the higher-ranked ape who initiates appeasing behaviors in order to repair the relationships with a lower hierarchy ape (De Waal 2000). However, in families where ongoing conflict has confused the hierarchal system and both parent and adolescents often feel powerless and paralyzed by shame, these shame reduction activities disappear, and instead, both sides adopt a passive "waiting position" for the other to make the first move.

When the parent-child relationship gets stuck in this way, it is the effect of others' opinions that can move the system forward. The best way of achieving this is to feed positive, caring, and hopeful opinions into the system. To do this, we ask parents to recruit people from their support system and have them deliver "anti-shame" messages to the child. These messages of respect include:

*Messages of pride in him* While shame is the sign of alienation and a facilitator of it, pride signals and generates solidarity (Scheff 1997). Hearing messages of pride after hearing criticism for so long has a huge impact on the adolescent. Messages, such as "I just wanted to let you know that I am proud of who you are/what you did," help the teen to feel less isolated and more connected to the parents' social group.

*Messages of his importance and specialness* Feeling special, unique, and important for others reduces shame (Gilbert 2007). Messages from the public, such as "in my eyes you are really special" or "To me, you are important," help adolescents to transcend the role of "being bad" and connect them with other more positive parts of themselves. It is important that others do not try to "convince" the adolescent that he has value. This only makes the teen feel worse and more alone. Instead, using the term "in my eyes" or "in my view" (…you are special) helps the teen to accept these messages without fearing that he is being required to change his own views about himself.

*Messages of hope* The process of shame regulation is not linear, but rather a rough and scary roller coaster ride. Relapses are common, giving everyone the feeling that this is a Sisyphean task. The ability of adolescent and parents to maintain hope and to not give up in face of these backslides depends on the amount of support and hope they receive from others. Simple statements like "There is hope," "You are doing a good job," or "Everything is ok" are tremendously helpful.

*Belonging messages* Shame-ridden adolescents often feel that they don't belong to their family or any other social group. After multiple experiences of rejection, they also believe that they can't belong. When they do eventually satisfy this need, it is often with the wrong crowd; their surrogate clique supports them in distancing themselves from their families and community. The ability of others within the teen's original "clan" to deliver him/her messages such as "You will always be one of us," "We are not giving up on you," and "We want you to participate in an event that is scheduled for…" has the potential of alleviating shame.

While, initially, there may be fear that such messages will negatively empower the adolescent or provide opportunities for non-constructive coalitions within the system, experience shows that such messages have the opposite effect. Communicating to both parent and adolescent variations of "There is hope; you are good; you are not alone." helps both parent and teen to move in those directions. When the public is advised that their only role is to generate these positive messages, and not to try to "save" the family, then such influence becomes more effective in bringing the two sides closer and in helping them to be their best.

Let's look at the example of a 14-year-old boy, David, whom I have been treating for the last 5 months. His school referred him to me because he refused to go to school for almost the whole year. This teen had immigrated to Israel from the USA a year before and had never found a way to fit in. During the year he became aggressive towards his parents and had very low motivation to achieve. In the first months of therapy, we worked intensively to reduce David's shame, and a big part of that intervention was endeavored through connecting him with others. These efforts were fruitful; David began the new school year and attended it regularly. However, the situation was far from calm. David's parents had to regulate his emotional outbursts daily. About a month after school began, David asked his parents to visit the Western Wall in Jerusalem. On their way there, he made unsuccessful attempts to get in touch with another kid from his class. This led David to feel like a failure

He thought that the other kid wasn't interested in his friendship. He began acting aggressively towards his parents. The parents, who were not aware of the phone call to the friend, were getting angry too. The father said he wanted to go back home, but the mother insisted that they continue. They went to the Western Wall, but as time passed David's behavior became worse. He shouted "I hate you! Why did you bring me to Israel?" and started pushing his father who was trying to control himself. The mother suddenly saw a policeman. She went to him and asked him to intervene. The policeman approached David and told him:

Policeman: "This is no way to behave towards your parents!"
David (angrily): "What do you know? Mind your own business."
Policeman (angrily and ashamed): "You watch your mouth when you talk to me!"
David: "I'll do what I want!"

Fearing further escalation, the mother then intervened and asked the policeman to leave. The parents, exhausted, wanted to go home, but David refused. Helpless, they sat around watching the many soldiers who were in the area.[3] David was still angry with his parents and with himself:

David: "Everything is bullshit. I really want to kill myself. I wish that one of these soldiers would come and kill me."

The parents and David were now sitting close to one of the army units. David spoke to his mother again:

David: "I wished they'd just shoot me so we could end all of this."

The mother noticed that the soldiers who were sitting next to them included a sergeant with an American accent. At a loss for what to do, she approached him and said with a smile:

Mother (to sergeant): "My son wants you to shoot him…."
Sergeant (surprised and baffled): "What?!"
Mother: "You heard me. My son told me that he wants to die, and he wants you to shoot him."
Sergeant (becoming curious): "Which is your son?"
Mother: "That kid over there."

The sergeant went over to David and had a short talk with him. Afterwards, David followed him and joined the other soldiers. "I don't know what he said to him; I think he just invited him to hang out with the soldiers in his unit." David sat with them for nearly an hour. The parents sat close by and took photos of the surprising group dynamics.

[3] In Israel everyone is drafted to the military, so the relationship between soldiers and citizens is close. During the Jewish New Year season, many army units go to the Western Wall for various ceremonies.

After an hour, David approached his parents and said that he wanted to go back home. The drive back home was calm. When they arrived home, the mother noticed that David was carrying a gift from the sergeant, a small patch with the symbol of their army unit, which David put next to his bed. The next day he woke up more energetic than usual.

Just as the policeman's involvement had caused an escalation in David's belligerent distress and alienation, the sergeant's involvement led David to calm down, feel connected, and feel a sense of worth. While the policeman had immediately lost his empathy towards David, the sergeant's empathetic stance had enabled David to regulate his shame.

## 6.7 Deshaming Communication

While intense shame states do not allow for deep conversations, communication does not cease completely. Yet whether out of the frustration or of despair, the little communication which is still present can tragically fuel additional shame cycles.

### *6.7.1 Reducing Criticism*

When adolescents experience intense shame, their lives are often marked by many failures. Whether the failures are academic, interpersonal, related to household chores, or any other type, they trigger parents to offer what they think are helpful corrections, explanations, and educational lectures. However, the adolescent actually experiences these as criticism, disapproval, and blame. Seemingly "neutral" comments such as "Please put your shoes back in their place," "Don't talk to me like that," and "If you continue to talk to your friends like that, they will leave you" can ignite a strong shame reaction.

The first step in reducing the adolescent's shame is a conscious decision by the parents to stop mentioning anything that might sound critical to the child. This often means that a very big chunk of the parent-adolescent interaction dissolves. I explain to parents that taking such a radical step is appropriate at times when their child is unable to tolerate any shame. If the parents insist that they need to correct the child, I answer, "I know that you care about your son, and that you want him to move forward and improve many aspects of his life. However, right now he is not able to tolerate any corrections. They are not helping him to move forward, and are actually intensifying the pain within him, and making him feel more like a failure." My aim is to free the teen from encounters where he experiences shame and fails to regulate it. When parents adopt such a position, it provides a balancing context to the shame evoking interventions of "sitting with shame" and "systemic exposure."

### 6.7.2 Communicating Without Shaming

In noncooperative states, parents feel that saying almost anything will lead the child to explode. This is often true, but there is a particular logic behind these outbursts. Let's take, for example, what feels like a caring question from the parents:

"How was your day in school?"
The adolescent answers harshly:
"Leave me alone and don't ask me any stupid questions!"

Why should such a question evoke such an extreme reaction? Because, by asking this question, the parent unknowingly evokes a shame-related theme in the teen's life. To help parents understand the true impact of their various behaviors, I often use the metaphor of pain. I explain to parents that their child is now suffering from intense pain. Any movement in the area of his injury will make him react like any injured person would, by attacking or by trying to run away. Still, this does not mean that parents need to give up on communicating with their child. Instead, parents can create interpersonal bridges to the child which do not involve evaluation, and which make it less likely that shame will be triggered. For example, statements such as "I'm thinking about you," "I love you," and "I'm sorry that we had a fight yesterday" create connections to the child without raising the shame level. Moreover, short sentences of this kind have a prophylactic function. They counter the tendency of shamed individuals to reach conclusions by incorrectly "mind reading" the other's intentions. By providing on-going information as to what is going through their minds, the parents are neutralizing the pain-related thoughts that shame is producing within their child.

### 6.7.3 Admitting and Apologizing

Just as adolescents need to feel appreciated and valued by their parents, so do parents need to feel valued by their children. Unfortunately, when both sides of a conflict feel insulted and disrespected, they each need the other person to make the first step before they can reciprocate. This problem is one of the major challenges in transforming negative and alienated interpersonal cycles into positive cycles (Wile 1993). Each side is saying to themselves, "Before I can admit my part, before I can apologize, before I can show appreciation and love for the other person, I need them to first do these things for me." Waiting for that to happen does not make things better. Instead, the longer it takes for one side to make a peace offering, the greater the chances that this gesture will not ameliorate the pain and will, instead, be experienced by the other as being "too little, too late."

The higher the shame state, the less chance the person will admit to his wrongdoing and apologize. It is unrealistic to expect teens who experience intense shame to apologize first. Instead, I coach parents on regularly admitting to their mistakes and apologizing for them (Weinblatt 2017). For example, I will advise the parent who, in an earlier example, asked "How was your day at school?" to apologize for that. If the parent replies, "She is the one that needs to apologize!", I answer, "That is true, but you also hurt him unintentionally." Such apologizing often leads to powerful shame regulation interactions:

Father: "I'm sorry I asked you about school, I know it upset you."
Daughter: "So why did you ask that, if you know it hurts me?"
Father: "Because I wanted to start a conversation with you. I only realized it was a stupid question after I asked it."
Daughter: "So next time you want us to talk, just say so."
Father: (smiling) "Sometimes I make things harder than they are."
Daughter: (smiling) "You are not the only one who does that, Dad…."

## References

Ahmed, E., Harris, N., Braithwaite, J., & Braithwaite, V. (2001). *Shame management through reintegration*. Melbourne: Cambridge University Press.
Armstrong, M. I., Birnie-Lefcovitch, S., & Ungar, M. T. (2005). Pathways between social support, family well-being, quality of parenting, and child resilience: What we know. *Journal of Child and Family Studies, 14*(2), 269–281.
Braithwaite, J. (1989). *Crime, shame and reintegration*. Cambridge University Press.
De Waal, F. B. (2000). Primates--a natural heritage of conflict resolution. *Science, 289*(5479), 586–590.
Gilbert, P. (2007). The evolution of shame as a marker for relationship security: A biopsychosocial approach. In J. L. Tracy, R. W. Robins, & J. P. Tangney (Eds.), *The self-conscious emotions: Theory and research* (pp. 283–309). New York: Guilford Press.
Gilligan, J. (2001). *Violence: A reflection on the National Epidemic*. New York: Pantheon Books.
Jacquet, J. (2015). Is shame necessary? New uses for an old tool. New York: Pantheon Books.
Omer, H. (2001). Helping parents deal with Children's acute disciplinary problems without escalation: The principle of nonviolent resistance. *Family Process, 40*(1), 53–66.
Omer, H. (2004). *Non-violent resistance: A new approach to violent and self-destructive children*. Cambridge: Cambridge University Press.
Omer, H., Weinblatt, U., & Kerwinkel, C. (2004). The parent manual. In H. Omer (Ed.), *Non-violent resistance: A new approach to violent and self-destructive children*. Cambridge: Cambridge University Press.
Potter-Efron, R. (2007). *Rage: A step-by-step guide to overcoming explosive anger*. Oakland: New Harbinger Publications.
Sanderson, C. (2015). *Counselling skills for working with shame*. London: Jessica Kingsley Publishers.
Scheff, T. J. (1997). *Emotions, the social bond, and human reality: Part/whole analysis*. New York, Cambridge University Press.
Shapiro, E. L., & Powers, T. A. (2011). Shame and the paradox of group therapy. In R. L. Dearing & J. P. Tangney (Eds.), *Shame in the therapy hour* (pp. 115–135). Washington, DC: American Psychological Association.
Smith, R. H., Webster, J. M., Parrott, W. G., & Eyre, H. L. (2002). The role of public exposure in moral and nonmoral shame and guilt. *Journal of Personality and Social Psychology, 83*(1), 138.

Tangney, J. P., Miller, R. S., Flicker, L., & Barlow, D. H. (1996). Are shame, guilt, and embarrassment distinct emotions? *Journal of Personality and Social Psychology, 70*(6), 1256.

Tangney, J. P., & Dearing, R. L. (2002). *Shame and guilt.* New York, NY: Guilford Press.

Tangney, J. P., Stuewig, J., & Mashek, D. (2007). Moral emotions and moral behavior. *Annual Review of Psychology, 58*, 345–372.

Tomkins, S. (1963). *Affect/imagery/consciousness, The negative affects* (Vol. 2). Oxford: England Springer.

Weinblatt, U., & Omer, H. (2008). Nonviolent resistance: A treatment for parents of children with acute behavior problems. *Journal of Marital and Family Therapy, 34*(1), 75–92.

Weinblatt, U. (2017). Sorry is the hardest word: Wie man Entschuldigungen nutzt, um Schamgefühle in Beziehungen zu mindern. *(How to use apologies in order to reduce shame) systhema, 31*(2), 122–135.

Wile, D. B. (1993). *After the fight: Using your disagreements to build a stronger relationship.* New York: Guilford Press.

Wurmser, L. (2000). *The power of the inner judge*. Northvale: Jason Aronson.

# Chapter 7
# Regulating Shame in Schools: All You Need Is Respect

Shame is everywhere in schools:

Teacher: "Michael, please open your book to page 9, and answer question number 1."

Not a sentence that you'd expect to stir up emotions. Yet, whenever there is a demand, there is potential for shame to appear. In the example above, the request made by the teacher places her, momentarily, in a higher hierarchical position than the student. Since shame is the emotion most associated with hierarchy and power (Gilbert 2000), this positioning evokes a shame response in the child. Children who have difficulty regulating shame will not respond cooperatively to such requests, viewing such collaboration as a sign of weakness, humiliation, and inferiority.

When students experience shame, they do one of two things: they either fight or withdraw. When fighting, students try to reduce their shame by transferring it to the teacher:

Michael: "Why don't *you* open *your* book?" (Class laughs)

And now it is the teacher who is feeling belittled, disrespected, and humiliated, and it is she who is saddled with the challenge of managing her shame.

The teacher's demand is not the only shame trigger in this situation. Let's assume, for example, that the student doesn't know how (or is not confident in his ability) to answer question number 1 correctly. The fear of being exposed as incompetent or as a failure (in the eyes of the teacher, classmates, and self) also activates a powerful shame reaction. In such circumstances, some students prefer withdrawing to fighting; they try to reduce their shame by hiding it:

Michael: "I don't have a book, I forgot it at home."

While this reaction is less damaging to the relationship than the combative response, it keeps the student's shame hidden and unapproachable and perpetuates the student's isolation.

Shame is ubiquitous in schools because three basic shame-related processes are constantly present:



U. Weinblatt, *Shame Regulation Therapy for Families*,
https://doi.org/10.1007/978-3-319-77470-1_7

- Evaluation: grading students and evaluating teacher's performance.
- Comparisons: examining one's abilities and achievements in contrast to what others have achieved (both students and teachers).
- Belonging: assessing whether one is part of the group, valued, and respected by other classmates (for students) or appreciated and esteemed by other educators (for teachers). That would include a wider group, like the principal and the school counselors, the parent-teacher committee, and board of education.

These three processes set the stage for student and teacher to be vulnerable and highly sensitive to experiencing shame and demand that both parties continually regulate their shame. The processes of evaluation, comparison, and belonging affect not only students and teachers but also the parents of the students. Parents feel evaluated by teachers (especially if the child is misbehaving at school or fails academically), compare their child to others (and to themselves as students), and can feel stigmatized or marginalized by other parents.

## 7.1 A Problem Called Problem Solving

Teachers are ordinarily taught that effective communication with kids who misbehave in the class revolves around problem solving. Although such conversations are useful in low shame states, when shame is the major factor fueling the problematic behavior, such conversations lead either to noncooperation or to promises which, if broken, lead to more disappointment and shame.

When a teacher and a student experience high levels of shame, their chances of having a constructive problem solving conversation with each other are slim. Such exchanges are often fights disguising themselves as conversations, or a conversation that lacks any emotional impact because the student is emotionally detached and disconnected. These swings between fighting and disconnection are typical of the effect that unregulated shame has on the communication process.

Yet, for shame to be neutralized, conversations are vital. The question is: what kind of conversation and in what format? In this chapter, I present two shame-sensitive conversations. The first conversation is based on the systemic mirroring format (counselor, teacher, and student), and the second involves a teacher and parents. While the conversations are different in structure, they are similar in style and intention, and both generate respectful interpersonal environments. Both focus on the following:

- "Solving the moment" instead of "solving the problem" (Wile 2011): viewing shame as the core problem and solving it through voicing that which shame has silenced (fears, wishes, other emotions)
- Using apologies freely: understanding that in high shame states, people are easily hurt and offended and that apologies can ease the pain generated by the conversation (Weinblatt 2017; Lazare 2005)

- Transparency of intent: selectively sharing thoughts that go through one's mind, thereby clarifying one's various intentions during the conversation. By doing so, one reduces communicative error (Asen and Fonagy 2012)
- Exposing one's own vulnerabilities in ways that humanize the person in the eyes of the other (Brown 2015)
- Understanding provocative/hostile statements as clues to the presence of shame
- Searching for ways to reveal one's own shame without shaming the other

## 7.2 A Relational Approach

When children misbehave in the classroom, interventions often focus on either the teacher's class management skills and projection of authority or the child's unruly conduct, leading to different behavioral interventions. While both approaches can be highly effective, they become less so when unregulated shame is involved. Shame is triggered within a relationship, and it is through the modification of this relationship that shame can be most profoundly regulated (DeYoung 2015).

The biggest challenge in working through a relational perspective lies in the fact that shame is often experienced by both the teacher and the student. As long as the teacher's experience of shame is below a certain threshold, she[1] can lead a fruitful conversation that will ease the shame of the student, as well as her own. But as shame becomes more intense, it becomes harder and riskier for teacher and student to talk directly. Such "conversations" can, in seconds, slip into verbal boxing matches, leaving both sides in a worse state than they were before the "talk." In such circumstances it is much more effective to have the conversation with a third person (school counselor or any professional experienced in relational work) who takes on the role of couple's therapist, aiming to improve the teacher-student relationship. This person's main focus should be stabilizing the relationship and helping teacher and student move closer to one another. In order to do so, both need to have a real conversation in which they open up and expose their vulnerabilities and weaknesses. In other words, they need to show their humaneness. That is never easy, especially when both teacher and student are experiencing painful shame that makes them feel weak and increases their urge to fight or to hide.

Nevertheless, working directly on the teacher-student relationship by meeting with the teacher and student together, and having a conversation with them about their relationship, is a very powerful tool in developing (within both student and teacher) the motivation to make more of an effort to help the other, developing more empathy towards the other, and strengthening their confidence in their abilities to achieve greater success with one another.

---

[1] Teacher and student could be of either gender, but for the sake of clarity in reading, I refer to teachers as female and students as male.

## 7.3 Having a Voice

Shame is the sentinel that guards the self, and like a triage nurse, it filters and prioritizes our awareness of various emotions, thoughts, and needs. As shame intensifies we lose the ability to perceive contextual information and the entirety of what is happening to us and instead become strongly focused on our pain and victimhood. This is part of the process I termed "loss of voice." To lose one's voice does not necessarily mean that one becomes silent (although this might also occur, typically, when all questions are answered with "I don't know"). Rather, when experiencing a loss of voice, people become more vocal: they scream and yell, criticize, give lectures, and – above all – blame. Yet this type of "voice" actually reflects the narrowing of experience. When losing voice, one loses the ability to express what is most influential and important in the moment; this means losing the ability to express wishes, fears, and vulnerable emotions (Wile 2011). The loss of voice leads to a loss of connection: a breakdown in the capacity of the teacher and student to communicate with one another, to seek each other's cooperation, and to care for each other.

Sometimes teachers and students find their voices, that is, they are suddenly able to communicate their true feelings, only to discover that the revelation has led to a disruption in the conversation. For example, during a talk a teacher tells the pupil:

> "I am angry."

While such words might represent the teacher's experience (reclaiming her voice), they can easily lead to a dynamic of hostility or disconnection if, for example, the student replies with the following:

- And I am angry with you!
- That is your problem!
- Or just remains silent

Such reactions are clues that the student is experiencing shame as a result of the teacher's statement. The message he's getting is "you are bad," and in general, he experiences the discussion as a fight and not as a conversation. So, experiencing sovereignty of voice is not enough to overcome disconnection; we need to add elements to that reclaimed voice, facets that will create and enhance connection with the other. Therefore, when the teacher says "I am angry," we intervene and attempt to voice a more comprehensive experience on behalf of the teacher, an experience which will enable connection with the student:

Counselor (to teacher) "I felt that behind those words "I am angry," there may lie some more words, and I want to voice them for you. So, did you mean to tell your student" (counselor shifting in seat, looking at student, and talking as if he were the teacher)":

> "I am angry *but I don't want it to interrupt the conversation we are having here.*"
> Or
> "I am angry *and I wish I wasn't angry.*"
> Or
> "I am angry *and I think you might be angry with me too.*"

The goal is to help the teacher have a voice, but one that will develop the conversation, create curiosity, and facilitate a sense of togetherness with the student. In other words, the counselor's goal is to seek out the missing conversation between the teacher and student, the conversation that will lead them forward as well as closer. When successful, such conversations have a huge impact on the teacher and student. After such conversations teachers often:

- Feel that they can handle the child better.
- Feel more in control.
- Develop empathy for the child.
- Allow themselves to use their full capacities and skill sets. They suddenly show more skillful management of the child.

The student often feels:

- Respected and that he was really understood
- Motivated to make an effort
- Empathy towards the teacher
- A sense of worth

And what these conversations do to shame is:

1. Reduce its destructive effects
2. Sometimes eliminate it entirely
3. Turn its presence into opportunities for closeness

Let us examine such a conversation. The following is a conversation I had with 15-year-old Kevin and his teacher Sara. Kevin was referred to me by his school. He had been missing classes frequently and interrupting classes he attended. After two sessions in which I met with him and his parents, I meet with him and his teacher at the school. Here, I present two conversations: the one I had with them and the one I simultaneously had with my own inner critic, a part of me that accuses me, blames me, and criticizes my work, in other words, the hidden conversation I had with my own shame. Through this double conversation, I wish to reveal the inner workings of shame on both the interpersonal and intrapersonal levels and the process of shame's regulation.

So, I'm sitting in a schoolroom with Kevin and his teacher, Sara.

Uri: So, tell me why we are meeting.

Teacher Sara: We have been having problems in class, a lot of disturbances, talking, and there has also been a lot of skipping classes.

The teacher thinks that she is sharing objective data. I think she is even making an effort to refrain from accusing Kevin by using the word "we" and by not blaming him directly. Yet, I am quite sure that Kevin experiences this as criticism and accusations that are intensifying his shame. He views this as the beginning of a fight and responds accordingly:

Kevin: And I am always the one who gets blamed; it's always my fault!

Teacher Sara: Sometimes it's your fault, and sometimes it's not.

Kevin: But why isn't Dan (another boy that interrupts the class) here; why's it me?
Teacher Sara: Because right now we are focusing on you.

What I wished the teacher had said is "because now we are talking about us, about how *we* can make things better between us," but that would have required the teacher to be vulnerable and open to the idea that this is a relational issue.

Uri's inner critic: But isn't the child the real problem?? Why sugarcoat it? He's misbehaving in the classroom, and he needs to "own" it!
Uri to critic: I think he knows it, and rubbing it in his face is not going to make him do anything about it. While I do agree with you that he needs to take responsibility for his actions, he is not the only one who needs to do that. That's why I wish the teacher had said "us"; that would have recognized them both as people who need to change and take responsibility. And when grown-ups take responsibility, it helps kids to do the same.
Kevin (to me): You see? It's always my fault!
Uri: Well, what I thought I heard your teacher say is "It's not about finding who's at fault, but rather, it's about how we, that is – you and I, can make things better". (Turning to face the teacher) Is that what you meant?
Teacher Sara: Yes, I didn't come here to blame him; I just want things to improve.
Kevin (to Uri): I want things to improve too, but do you know that 2 weeks ago she kicked me out of class and said "I want you out of my class forever?"
Teacher Sara (embarrassed): That is not exactly what I said. What I said was….

I interrupt the conversation because they are heading into a "who-said-what-conversation." That never leads to anything good, so I jump in again:

Uri (to teacher): I thought that what Kevin was really trying to say was "That day when you said you don't want me in your classroom, I didn't deserve that."
Uri's inner critic: What the hell are you doing Uri!? You're building a coalition with the student against the teacher?! He will take advantage of it and accuse her of even more and feel more entitled! I think you just made a big mistake here.
Uri to critic: You are right that I just positioned myself on Kevin's side, but I also think that you are overreacting a little bit. In a minute, I will be on the teacher's side and then on his and so on. In order for Kevin to expose his feelings, he needs to feel safe; he needs someone on his side.
Uri's inner critic: I really hope you know what you are doing….
Teacher Sara: I didn't have a choice. You were interrupting the class and I had repeatedly and nicely asked you to stop. And it continued and continued.
Kevin: So maybe I shouldn't be in the class!
Uri's inner critic: Ha ha, I win! You see, now he is going to think that it is ok to cut classes and ditch school!
Uri to inner critic: I don't think this is a power issue. I think that Kevin doesn't believe that he can be successful in school. It's unfortunate that he can't communicate that. But that's what shame does to all of us. It is my work to voice that despair without alienating the teacher.

Uri (to Kevin): You said something important and I want to voice it. Let me know if I'm heading in the right direction, ok?

Kevin: ok

Uri (to teacher): What I heard in Kevin's last sentence was, "I am not sure that I can be successful in class and stop interrupting, so the solution I have in my mind right now is to stop going to school." (To Kevin) Is it something like that?

Kevin: Yes, more or less.

Uri: Can you say more; can you expand on what I just said?

Kevin: Yah, sometimes I make a decision to stop interrupting, sometimes I tell myself I'll stop interrupting, but then I find myself doing it again.

Uri (to teacher): And what is your reaction to this?

Teacher Sara: I'm sorry he feels that he shouldn't be in the class, but that's not a good solution.

Kevin: You suggested it yourself!

The teacher was softening up, but Kevin's last remark is provocative. That means I must intervene quickly. I view his last remark as a sign or a clue that he is still hurt by the teacher's remark that he shouldn't be in class. However, now he's managed to turn that hurt into a weapon, something that empowers him. So, our first task is to bring closure to that event.

Uri's inner critic: Don't tell me that you are going to make the teacher apologize for that!

Uri to critic: Not "make" but help the teacher to apologize for that. Apologies are crucial in the process of shame management. In this case, I want to help the teacher to apologize, not only to reduce Kevin's shame but her own as well. I know she is sorry for what she said. I know she would prefer to have said something else. I know she is experiencing shame about the issue, and I want to relieve her of that. So, before she can reply to his provocative sentence I say:

Uri to Kevin: What I thought your teacher tried to communicate earlier was "I do not want you out of my class. I wish I hadn't said that, and that I hadn't hurt you."

Uri (to Teacher): Would you agree with that?

Teacher Sara: Yes, I don't want him out of class. I should not have said what I said, and we really need to find ways to avoid getting into the same situation again.

Uri (to teacher): And now I want to expand on what you just said. (Looking at Kevin) If I had been your teacher, I might feel like "I know it wasn't right to say those words, but you also hurt me by disturbing the class. I felt like you didn't respect me." (Looking now at the teacher) Is this part of your experience?

Teacher Sara: Yes, it felt like he didn't care about what I say. I got angry because I am really trying to help Kevin, and by interrupting it felt like he doesn't appreciate it.

Uri critic: I think you have led the teacher to open up too much. Students do not need to know that they hurt their teachers. They will think of them as weak teachers. Teachers need to show their strength, not to show as much vulnerability as the child.

Uri to critic: I think what you are feeling is fear. And let me reveal something to you – part of the problem stems from teachers acting as if they are not hurt. That way, students can never develop empathy towards them. I am not suggesting that teachers disclose their emotions in damaging ways or expose themselves in ways that make them look as though they've lost control. But in a one-on-one conversation, this admission of vulnerability is very helpful to both sides. In order for Kevin to really understand the impact of his behavior, he needs to feel the teacher's pain. Otherwise, the conversation is not a real one.

Kevin: (whispering) That wasn't my intention....

Uri (to Kevin): I want to turn what your teacher just said into a question: Did you know that you hurt me when you didn't respond to my requests?

Uri's inner critic: I think your approach is very risky. What happens if he answers, "yes I wanted to hurt you"?

Uri to inner critic: Then I'd work with that; I'd say to the student:

"Let me try to guess and expand on what you just said. Did you really mean 'I wanted to hurt you' because:

(a) I felt disrespected by you, or
(b) Because I don't want you to have any expectations of me, or
(c) Something else completely?"

I am giving the student a chance to explore various possible reasons for his behaviors. Most people, including students, want to hurt others because they've felt humiliated, belittled, or inferior themselves. We often view adolescents with behavioral problems as people whose main goal is to hurt others. This is usually not the case. And from what I observed of Kevin, he's not malicious. However, adolescents do act in ways that seem disconnected and shameless. This is often the result of intense shame, which disconnects the adolescent from himself and from others.

Kevin: I am sorry....

Teacher Sara: It's o.k., you don't need to apologize. It's just that we need to think about how we're going to prevent this from happening again.

What I wish the teacher had said here was a simple "thank you." That would have maintained the intimate moment between them. But the teacher, for some reason, didn't feel comfortable with this closeness. I often hear this sentence: "I don't need an apology, I just need...", and then the conversation turns into another problem-solving conversation. Kevin doesn't need this type of conversation because he already knows what he needs to do. He needs to do his best to maintain concentration and to participate in the class like any other student. And I imagine that by now he has ideas as to how he can do that. The problem is that he is not making enough of an effort to do those things. That is because he doubts his own abilities and because the relationship with the teacher is not one that is motivating him to try harder. And that is exactly my goal: to help Kevin want to change; to develop his desire for something different; and to develop his courage to invest effort without knowing for sure that he is going to be successful. In my experience, developing such an attitude is often the result of developing a certain kind of relationship between the teacher and student and not necessarily the result of an individual's unilateral decision which is made in a relational void.

My goal is to create an experience in which each side wants to make more of an effort for the other and in which each side sees the efforts others make on their behalf. Often, this means managing the shame that is connected to these actions. Then, when shame is reduced and the person really sees those efforts made for them by the other, significant changes occur in the motivational level of both sides.

Let me provide examples from other relational contexts. A couple I had been treating would argue endlessly about cleaning issues. She was cleaner and more organized than he was. Their fights would escalate into vicious power struggles. Each side felt disrespected and not appreciated by the other. After a couple of months of therapy, they felt much better and thought they'd had enough. In the final session, I asked the wife what had changed, and the wife answered with a smile "He's still a dirty pig but now he is really making an effort to be cleaner." Another example: a couple had a terrible fight in session. I did everything possible to calm things down, but to no avail. They left the session in worse condition than when they entered. The next week I met with them, I told them that I was really sorry for how the last session ended and that it is my responsibility that they don't end a session in so much pain. The wife looked at me and said "Don't worry about it Uri; it's ok. At least you tried."

So, when Kevin says "I am sorry," and he says it sincerely, I see the seeds that can germinate into real efforts made on his part. Thus, instead of going into a problem-solving conversation (which the teacher's last remark is leading us to), I try to maintain the moment of emotional connection by moving the teacher closer to Kevin. I do so by saying:

Uri (to teacher): I want to expand a bit what you just said, and then let me know whether this fits with your experience, o.k.?

Techer Sara: ok

Uri (to Kevin): I thought your teacher's main point was, "Thank you for saying that you are sorry. I guess we both need to work hard in order to move forward."

Uri (to teacher): How much of this fits how you feel, and how much of it doesn't?

Teacher Sara: Yes, I am willing to put in the effort. Actually, I have already started. I made some changes in the classroom, moved students, and talked with the students about how we can respect one another. I believe that Kevin is aware of these changes.

The teacher is saying something quite remarkable, which is a result of the conversation we are having:

1. She is saying that she will make more of an effort. I think she is saying this because she recognizes the effort that Kevin is making at this moment.
2. She is admitting that Kevin is not the only problem. In the beginning of the meeting, she couldn't have said this because of the shame she felt. She felt too vulnerable, and she was afraid that saying so would have empowered Kevin in a negative way.

To be fair, there is a good chance that it would have, but now the situation is different. Now the teacher and Kevin have entered into what the psychologist Dan Wile calls an "admitting-admitting cycle" (Wile 1993) which leads both to be "on the platform," meaning that they are conjointly standing in an elevated position and are looking at the problem together from above it. This is precisely the relational dynamic that leads to the regulation of shame. Still, I wish that she had turned her last words into a question. Since she didn't, I'll do it for her:

Uri (to teacher): You said a few interesting things, but if its ok, I would like to turn your last sentence into a question. (Turning to Kevin) The question I heard from your teacher is, "Have you noticed the changes that I started implementing in the class?"
Kevin: Yes, I noticed; she spoke about changing the climate of the class.
Uri (to Kevin): And what are your thoughts about that?
Kevin: I guess it's good to try something new.
Teacher Sara: I'm happy he's saying this.
Student Kevin: Why?
Teacher Sara: Because it shows me that you care.

What I want to add now is, "because it shows that you care about *me*," but I don't want to overexpose the teacher.

Uri (to Kevin): And what are your thoughts right now?
Kevin: (shy smile) "ok…"

Kevin is saying little, but not because he's avoiding or experiencing loss of voice. Rather, he's busy making sense of this conversation and assimilating the new relationship. I can almost hear the wheels in his mind operating. For me, the point we have reached is satisfactory. The admitting-admitting cycle is an unstable state, which can be derailed by a strong shame reaction, for example, if Kevin had, instead of smiling and saying "ok," said:

"You see, I told you that it wasn't all about me; there are many problems in the classroom."

In such a case, we would have catapulted out of the admitting-admitting cycle and into another fight-or-withdraw-shame cycle. When the shame of the participants is very high, this kind of backsliding follows. Therefore, the conversation needs to continue in order for it to return to a positive cycle; there is need of more guided/therapeutic conversations of this sort.

But, luckily for all of us, Kevin is experiencing his teacher's last remarks as conciliatory. What he is hearing is "I know you are not the only one who needs to change. There are many problems in the classroom. You are not the worst student, and I am not a perfect teacher." This subtle taking of responsibility by the teacher is mirroring a reality that Kevin can relate to. By the teacher admitting to her lack of perfection, she is helping him to admit to his own weaknesses.

Kevin (to Uri): You know, now I am sitting in the front row with all the nerds! She thinks I'll be quiet up there with them….
Teacher Sara (smiling to Kevin): Kevin, I really don't think there is any danger of you becoming a nerd….

This sounds like a good ending, so I say:

Uri: Ok, thank you both for this good conversation. Would it be ok with you if we were to have another one in the future?

Uri inner critic: This sounds like psychobabble to me. I don't understand; what exactly have you achieved here? What is going to be different? What is the plan? And what are the consequences if Kevin continues to misbehave?

Uri to inner critic: If Kevin misbehaves, we'll meet again. And in that meeting, I will try to do the same, that is, help both teacher and student to reclaim voice, while at the same time strengthening their relationship. Relationships have lives and, as such, can be impacted by many factors. If Kevin misbehaves again, it could be for many different reasons:

- He might have lost hope.
- He might be experiencing self-doubts.
- He might be angry with the teacher.
- He might have fought with his friends.
- He might have come to school with a bad mood because of a fight with his parents.

And so on. What I am saying is that many of the conflictual situations we're dealing with are dynamic and take on a life of their own. Viewing them as static problems is fallacious and unhelpful. In our conversation, I intentionally refrained from developing a plan. I was content with the motivational or emotional shift that the two had experienced. Talking about a plan can easily destroy this motivation, create distance between the two again, and devalue the achievements that were gained.

Uri's critic: I don't know, I still have my doubts about you.

Uri to inner critic: That's fine. And as you well know there is no plan, no structure, no intervention that will make us silence the other, or that will completely solve the problem we have with one another. At the same time, our ability to talk to one another without escalating is something that I am proud of. We somehow managed to blend our differences into our relationship. We turned the differences between us into something manageable without becoming enemies. While we still have our differences, we can tolerate each other more, understand where each one of us is coming from, laugh at each other's mistakes, and, sometimes, even kind of like each other.

## 7.4 Regulating Shame in Teacher-Parent Meetings

When a teacher and parents meet to discuss a child's problematic behavior or poor academic achievements, the level of shame in the encounter is often high, even before a single word has been spoken. Parents have many reasons to feel ashamed:

- They are experiencing the shame of their inability or failure to influence their child to do better at school.

- They are experiencing the shame that is a result of "what others are thinking about us." They believe that school personnel think negatively about them because of their child's behavior.
- They might be experiencing shame as a result of previous embarrassing or humiliating encounters at school and the accumulative effect that this new encounter brings when combined with those.

Teachers too have many reasons to feel ashamed:

- The child might have disrespected and insulted them.
- They are failing to teach and educate the child effectively.
- They also might be carrying a painful history of previous shameful meetings with parents and their accumulative effect when combined with this one.

These high levels of preexisting shame place the parents and the teacher in a state of great vulnerability that breeds defensive misinterpretation. Neutral and even positive remarks can be interpreted as put-downs, problem-solving efforts as ways of controlling, and silences as noncooperation.

To highlight how tragically easy it is to fall into these shame traps, I would like to present a conversation between Sharon, the teacher of 12-year-old Jonathan, and his parents, Peter and Anna. Jonathan has been disturbing class lessons, unwilling to do assignments in the classroom, and often hasn't done his homework. Finally, the teacher invites the parents for a conference:

Teacher Sharon: Thank you for coming. I would like to talk to you about how Jonathan has been doing in school lately. But first, it is important for me to tell you that I find Jonathan to be an intelligent and friendly child and that he is well liked by many other students. Unfortunately, problems have been showing up recently; he has been disturbing the class and repeatedly shirking his homework.

The teacher begins with a constructive tone, hoping to emphasize Jonathan's positive traits. While this is a good effort, it is often not enough to regulate high levels of shame that are already present in the room. Before she can continue, the father interrupts her:

Father: How long has this been going on?
Teacher Sharon: About a month.
Father: Why weren't we notified earlier?

While the father's question can sound informative, it can also quickly trigger a shame response in the teacher. For example, if the teacher were to interpret the father's question as rhetorical, and as the accusation "You should have informed us earlier. The fact that you didn't makes you a bad teacher!", she would experience a painful shame reaction. The father on the other hand is not aware of how his questions are impacting the teacher. Actually, these questions are clues that he is experiencing shame at the moment and trying to regulate it. Unfortunately, his efforts to regulate his own shame are causing the teacher, Sharon, to experience shame.

So, the conversation has just started, and Sharon, who entered the meeting with the best of intentions, is already in a shaky position. Almost any answer she gives could increase the parents' own shame. For example, if she were to say:

> "I did inform you."
> or
> "It is your job and your responsibility to know."

She would add more fuel to the combustion of shame escalation.

When shame is present, it needs to be addressed quickly and with respect. Otherwise, it can rapidly transform the meeting into a destructive power struggle. Therefore, the opening phrases of a parent-teacher conference are essential in regulating the shame residing in both sides (and had been even before entering the meeting). If the teacher had started with:

> "Thank you for coming. I know that for some parents, meeting with teachers in school is not a pleasant experience. I will do everything possible to make this meeting a positive one. My only request is that if, during the conversation, you feel uncomfortable with something I say, you let me know please, ok?"

She would have had a better chance in regulating the shame in the room, because she would have addressed it. But Sharon, who is an excellent teacher, started differently, and now she can feel the tension in the room rising. If she were really at her best (i.e., if her shame were fully regulated), she could answer the father with the following words:

> "You are right. I should have gotten in touch with you earlier. I thought Jonathan's difficulties were temporary. I also thought that I could solve the problem alone without bothering you. I'm trying to help him, but I now realize that I will probably need your support in doing so."

Such a response from her would have probably evoked a positive response from the parents.

Unfortunately, Sharon is not at her best, for she began to experience shame. Nonetheless, she tries to conceal her shame and to sound (in her view) positive:

Teacher Sharon: The purpose of this meeting is to move Jonathan forward, not to blame anybody.

However, the mother does not recognize the teacher's effort to remain positive, for what she hears is "You shouldn't be blaming; you are bad!", a statement that increases her shame and leads her to reply with the following sentence:

Mother: We are not looking to blame anybody, we just do not understand why Jonathan's problems intensified this year. Last year he did so well....

Teacher Sharon's situation is growing worse, and now she is starting to take offense at what the mother is saying. Suddenly, she finds herself reflecting on all the things she did for Jonathan, things for which she received no recognition. Now, a big part of her does not want to remain positive. Feeling hurt, what she wants to say is:

"For all I care, he can go back to last year's teacher."
or
"I actually know that last year there were many problems as well."
or
"Maybe you parents were more involved last year, and this year you are less involved."

But deep down she knows that all these statements will only escalate the situation. What she needs is someone on her side, someone who will remind her that she is a good teacher. Luckily, she recalls a conversation she had with two colleagues just before the meeting with the parents. They had complemented her on her work. Being in touch with this memory makes Sharon feel less confused, less vulnerable, and more empathic. Remembering who she really is leads her back to being at her best:

Teacher Sharon: I am sorry that this year is not as successful as last year was. I would really like Jonathan to succeed. I will speak with teachers from last year to see what they did differently.

In these words, Sharon is doing something very significant in regard to shame management:

- She admits her own difficulties with Jonathan.
- She takes responsibility for her side of the problem, but not in a way that reduces theirs.
- She validates the parents' experience regarding last year.
- She is communicating to the parents that she is taking their concerns seriously.
- She is demonstrating caring.

Teacher Sharon's ability to admit, take responsibility, communicate openly, validate, and demonstrate care leads the parents to be able to do the same:

Mother: Actually, the truth is that last year Jonathan did get into some trouble….
Father: We also don't know how to motivate him.

Now the parents and the teacher are in an admitting-admitting cycle. Being in such a position is always the result of shame being regulated. When people reach this position, they become motivated, energized, and hopeful:

Teacher Sharon: I am sure that working together we can help Jonathan to advance.
Father: So, what do you propose to do, and how can we help?

And now the relationship between teacher and parents is one that allows for problem solving: each side's proposals for moving Jonathan forward will be evaluated according to their degree of feasibility and without the fear that the problem solving brainstorm will induce a strong shame reaction.

The ability to have a problem-solving conversation demands that participants have their shame regulated. In the former example, it was the carefully worded outreach from the teacher to the parents that led to an interpersonal state in which searching for solutions is possible. The same holds true in situations in which teachers experience an impasse in their relationship with a student. As the student's problems in the classroom increase, there is an ever-stronger tendency to focus conversations on the search for solutions. More often than not, this process will intensify the shame that is already intense. In such situations, adapting a shame-sensitive approach, which uses conversations as means for easing and managing shame, shifts the teacher, parents, and student from investing in adversarial or disconnected encounters to investing in ones that evoke hope.

## References

Asen, E., & Fonagy, P. (2012). Mentalization-based therapeutic interventions for families. *Journal of Family Therapy, 34*, 347–370.

Brown, B. (2015). *Daring greatly: How the courage to be vulnerable transforms the way we live, love, parent, and lead.* New York: Penguin.

DeYoung, P. A. (2015). *Understanding and treating chronic shame: A relational/neurobiological approach.* New York: Routledge.

Gilbert, P. (2000). The relationship of shame, social anxiety and depression: The role of the evaluation of social rank. *Clinical Psychology & Psychotherapy, 7*(3), 174–189.

Lazare, A. (2005). *On apology*. Oxford University Press.

Weinblatt, U. (2017). Sorry is the hardest word: Wie man Entschuldigungen nutzt, um Schamgefühle in Beziehungen zu mindern. *(How to use apologies in order to reduce shame) systhema, 31*(2), 122–135.

Wile, D. B. (1993). *After the fight: Using your disagreements to build a stronger relationship.* New York: Guilford Press.

Wile, D. B. (2011). Collaborative couple therapy: Turning fights into intimate conversations. *Psychotherapy in Australia, 17*(3), 52.

# Index





U. Weinblatt, *Shame Regulation Therapy for Families*,
https://doi.org/10.1007/978-3-319-77470-1

www.ingramcontent.com/pod-product-compliance
Lightning Source LLC
Chambersburg PA
CBHW071351230926
51846CB00002B/515
* 9 7 8 3 0 3 0 0 8 4 6 3 9 *